Quality Management 2000:
Preparing the Quality Improvement
Professional for the Future

Deborah K. Wall RN, BSN, MA
Mitchell M. Proyect, BA, SD

Precept Press, Chicago
Division of Bonus Books, Inc.

Wall, Deborah K.
    Quality management 2000: preparing the quality improvement professional
for the future / Deborah K. Wall, Mitchell M. Proyect.
        p.   cm.
    Includes biographical references and index.
    ISBN 0-944496-51-2 (alk. paper)
    1. Medical care–Quality control. 2. Medical care–Evaluation. 3. Health
services administration. I. Proyect, Mitchell M. II. Title.
RA394.W353   1997
362.1'068'5–dc21   97-23808
                                                                                CIP

Precept Press
Division of Bonus Books, Inc.
160 East Illinois Street
Chicago, Illinois 60611

Table of Contents

1

Health Care 2000

The only thing in health care that is not changing is the spelling of the words health care. For the past ten years, the industry has been in a constant state of flux while trying to provide high quality patient care with dwindling financial and human resources, evolving technologies and changing regulations. These trends are expected to continue and even accelerate during the next ten years, resulting in a radically different health care landscape. What will this new industry look like? What skills will be required to survive as a quality management professional?

To try to answer these questions, this book will explore:

- Identifying the economic, political and social factors which impact the health care system
- Identifying how the quality professional's role will change during the next ten years
- Describing what skills are required to meet future health care system quality, resource and safety needs
- Assessing his/her own ability to perform quality management in the future

Factors Influencing Health Care Trends

To answer these questions, let's explore the economic, social and technical factors impacting the health care system.

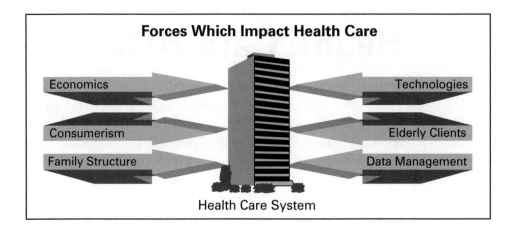

Forces Which Impact Health Care

Economics

Technologies

Consumerism

Elderly Clients

Family Structure

Data Management

Health Care System

Economics

Of all the forces influencing the health care industry, economics is the most powerful. It has caused major changes in what, where and how care is provided to patients. Between 1950 and 1987, health care expenditures grew from 4.4 percent to 11.1 percent of the gross national product.

In 1992, health care spending reached 14 percent of the gross domestic product and is expected to reach 19 percent by the year 2000. Because of this phenomenal growth, the healthcare industry has come under close scrutiny by consumers, employers, third-party payers and legislators. Each group is searching for a way to contain costs while preserving quality care and promoting better access.

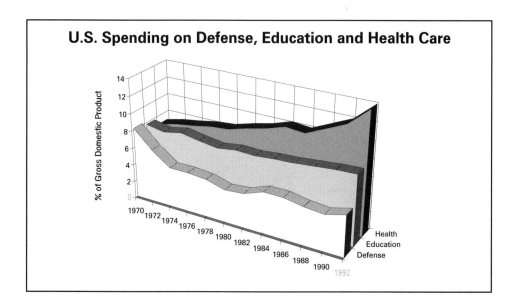

Consumerism

Renewed interest in consumerism surfaced in the 1960's and was captured in a speech on consumerism by President John F. Kennedy to Congress in 1962. This speech outlined the basic tenets of consumer rights which consisted of :

- The right to safety
- The right to be heard
- The right to be informed
- The right to choose

These basic rights significantly impact the health care industry through the development of safety regulations and consumer demands.

Accompanying the increased awareness of consumer rights, there has been a shift in consumers' expectations of the American health care system. A national poll in 1989 demonstrated that 89 percent of Americans believe the U.S. health care system needs fundamental change. Thus, there are simultaneous pressures to expand and retract the health care system and to expand services for certain groups such as the elderly, the uninsured and the poor while keeping costs within general inflationary pressures.

Above all else, the 1990s will be the decade of accountability at all levels—federal, state and local, and in both the public and private sectors. The new accountability player is, of course, private industry. Purchasers have gained great power relative to providers.

Consumerism Impacts the Health Care Industry

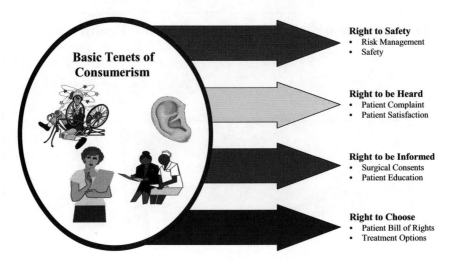

Private payers will join with government payers in holding providers accountable for both the cost and overall quality of performance, while emphasizing value added. The data underpinning such systems will come from measurements of patient outcome, treatment effectiveness and quality of care research. Providers who can deliver the goods will become well known for their abilities.

To understand how consumer power impacts the health care industry, one must recognize the framework for analyzing industries. The major dimensions to consider are the bargaining power of buyers, bargaining power of suppliers, substitutes for one's products or services, threat of new entrants into the market and the nature and intensity of competition among firms within the industry.

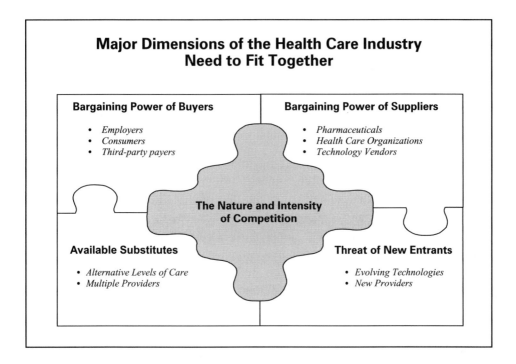

**Major Dimensions of the Health Care Industry
Need to Fit Together**

Bargaining Power of Buyers

- *Employers*
- *Consumers*
- *Third-party payers*

Bargaining Power of Suppliers

- *Pharmaceuticals*
- *Health Care Organizations*
- *Technology Vendors*

**The Nature and Intensity
of Competition**

Available Substitutes

- *Alternative Levels of Care*
- *Multiple Providers*

Threat of New Entrants

- *Evolving Technologies*
- *New Providers*

The two major health policy themes in the 1990s will be:

1. Tough choices based on value added and

2. Accountability for choices

Given the budget deficit and the growing fiscal uncertainty, resources flowing to the health care sector will be carefully scrutinized. Because of the increased clout by consumers, many changes in the health care delivery system have already been initiated.

Family Structure

Another societal factor impacting the health care system is the current family structure. This basic unit has changed dramatically during the past 20 years. Some of the characteristics of these changes include:

- Growing incidence of two-income families
- Increasing mobility of families
- Rising child and spouse abuse rates

These changes have a profound effect on the health care industry. For example, in the past, a person having a bowel resection could go home to recuperate with the help of family members. Now, because of the changes in the family structure, patients are now seeking outside help from extended care facilities and home health agencies.

Based on these family structure changes and the needs created, many new programs and organizations have sprung up to meet the health needs.

Aging Population

One of the fastest growing populations in the United States is the elderly. This population has been increasing since the turn of the century and will continue to increase through the first half of the next century. It can be safely predicted that by the next century every other adult patient seen by primary care physicians will be geriatric. Couple this increasing population with the fact that the elderly use more health care services than younger people and the result will be even greater demands on the health care system.

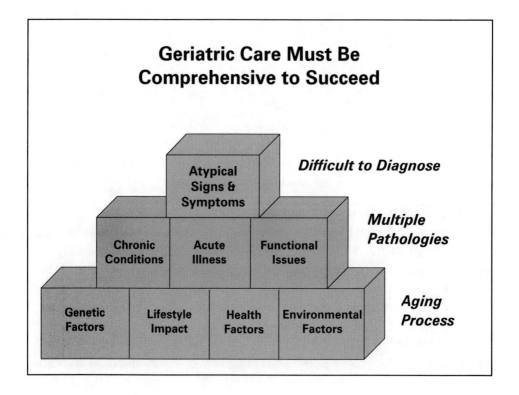

Technologies

Besides the economic and social factors which are shaping the health care industry, no discussion would be complete without mentioning the role of evolving technologies. Because of the development of sophisticated diagnostic and therapeutic technologies, patients are able to obtain care faster and safer with better results.

One of the most important technological advances is the development of information management technologies. The intent of this statement is not to underplay the importance of scientific breakthroughs and advances in diagnostic and therapeutic technologies, but to acknowledge the potential impact information will have on existing organizational and industrial structure.

Information Management Technologies

**Links Activities Together
Facilitates Standardization of Processes**

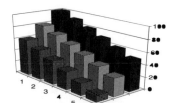

**Promotes Decision Making
Increases Data Analysis Abilities**

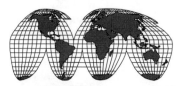

**Expands the Universe by Shrinking the World
Standardizes Language**

**Changes Possibilities to Probabilities
????????**

The Health Care System's Response

Many changes are occurring as a result of the internal and external pressures being placed on the health care industry. These changes consist of:

- Method of reimbursement
- Expansion of group physician practices
- Consolidation of health care organizations
- Compression of bureaucracies
- Development of alternate levels of care
- Creation of practice standards and guidelines
- Emphasis on quality of care
- Creation of clinical information management systems
- Revision of regulations

These nine trends can be grouped into four main categories: reimbursement strategies, institutional restructuring, alternate care expansion and quality/resource initiatives.

Health Care System's Response to External Forces

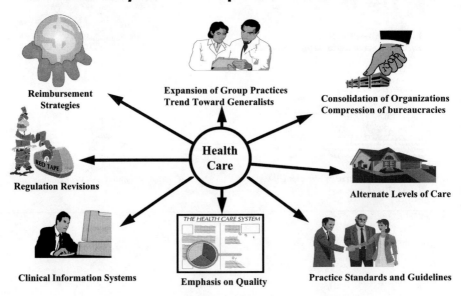

Reimbursement Strategies

Since 1965, there have been major changes in the reimbursement strategies for health care. Payment strategies have progressed from fee-for-service to prospective payment to capitated funding. It is estimated that by 1999 more than 70 percent of all hospitals' total revenues will be from capitated payment plans.

Reimbursement Strategies

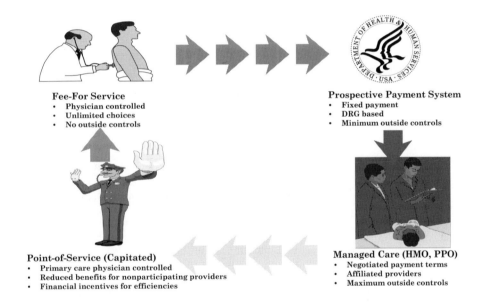

Fee-For Service
- Physician controlled
- Unlimited choices
- No outside controls

Prospective Payment System
- Fixed payment
- DRG based
- Minimum outside controls

Point-of-Service (Capitated)
- Primary care physician controlled
- Reduced benefits for nonparticipating providers
- Financial incentives for efficiencies

Managed Care (HMO, PPO)
- Negotiated payment terms
- Affiliated providers
- Maximum outside controls

Based on the reimbursement trends found during the past 20 years, the year 2000 will find capitated payment plans the dominant form of reimbursement. This model will be managed by primary care physicians and members of large group practices rather than insurance companies. Because physicians will have a vested interest in cost effective medical services and bargaining power regarding where patients will receive care, they will control the majority of health care dollars. Physician groups will enter into contracts with other health care organizations to provide care for a designated number of members at a capitated monthly fee.

There will be two dominant forms of physician practice models, one in which the health care facility will employ physicians, such as the Kaiser Permanente or the Veterans Affairs Medical System. The other model consists of physicians bonding together in a large group practice for bargaining power in managed care contracts. **Regardless of the model, the independent practitioner will become virtually extinct.**

Institutional Restructuring

Because of increasing demands by buyers and the need to provide a continuum of services, there is an increased rate of hospital, homecare, extended care and physician groups forming alliances, networks and systems. This trend can be expected to continue well into the next century. The result of this consolidation is a balance between the power of the buyer and the power of the supplier.

In addition to organizations merging, they are re-evaluating their present bureaucratic structure. Many organizations, especially those already participating in managed care programs, are flattening their organizations. This reduction of middle management positions is made possible by the use of information technologies and re-organization of functions. To help facilitate this re-organization, many administrators are turning to the concepts of reengineering.

Institutional Restructuring Flattens Organizations

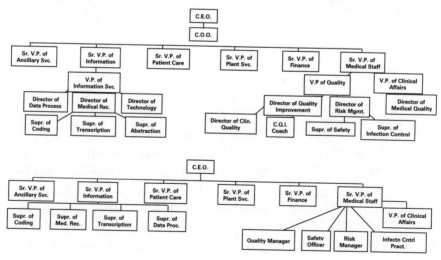

Alternate Care Expansion

With consumer demand for cost-effective care and the changes in the existing family structure, the health care industry has risen to meet these challenges with an expansion of alternate level of care organizations. Increases in the number of home health agencies, extended care facilities, hospices, adult day care centers, wellness programs and others are well known. This expansion has fostered a need for smooth transitions through the continuum of care. The roles of discharge planners and case managers have emerged within the health care industry to facilitate the required coordination between levels of care.

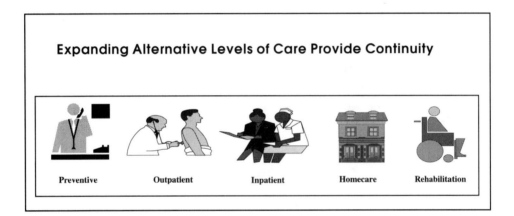

Expanding Alternative Levels of Care Provide Continuity

| Preventive | Outpatient | Inpatient | Homecare | Rehabilitation |

Quality/Resource Initiatives

Another response to increasing demand for accountability by consumers and legislation is the development of continuous quality improvement processes, expansion of patient care review activities and revision of accreditation and licensing standards. These efforts focus on improving the quality provided and controlling health care costs.

Quality and Resource Initiatives

Emphasis on Quality
Continuous Quality Improvement
Reengineering

Report Card	
Access	1
Quality	1.5
Safety	1.7
Overall	1.4

Accountability for Care
Outcome Measurements

JCAHO   NCQA

Changes in Regulations and Standards
Fight for Control of Accreditation

Pathways
Policies & Procedures
Practice Guidelines
& Standards

Development of Guidelines
Critical Pathway Movement

The New Quality Management Professionals

With all the changes occurring within the health care industry, what is expected of quality management professionals? How will their roles change over the next five to 10 years? What skills will be required to survive the new demands? Answers to these questions will be explored throughout this book.

The changes which quality management professionals can expect in the near future include:

- **Integration of monitoring processes** is inevitable with the requirement of cross-functional processes. Quality, resource and risk management responsibilities will be combined with discharge planning and infection control surveillance. Quality management professionals will be expected to be multi-tasking and able to coordinate patient care between levels of care.

- **Decentralization of data collection and case management personnel** will coincide with a centralization of data analysis functions. This change will support the trend toward "patient-focused" care and will be made possible with the development of sophisticated data management systems. Decision support systems will filter the enormous quantity of data in automated patient record repositories and focus attention on the information that really makes a difference.
- **Movement of quality management** positions from acute care to alternative levels of care will occur. This shift is due to the expansion of accreditation programs, shifts in patient distribution and regulatory changes in homecare, extended care, physician group practices, etc.
- **Standardization of clinical processes** will be widespread throughout the industry. This standardization will be based on the results of clinical and financial data analysis. To support the development, implementation and application of clinical guidelines and pathways, quality management professionals will need to be proficient in clinical study design, clinical and financial data analysis, project management, reengineering principles, adult education concepts, system analysis, change theory, conflict management and interpersonal skills. This minimum skill set will replace the current minimum of criteria application, chart analysis, accreditation standards expertise, patterning and trending ability and communication skills.

To determine readiness for the new quality management role and responsibilities, a readiness self-assessment was developed. Take a few minutes to determine your readiness to survive the paradigm shifts which are occurring in the health care industry.

Readiness Assessment Exercise

Directions: After reading the statement in the first column, select the level of performance which most closely matches your current knowledge, skills and abilities. Mark your answer in the appropriate box with a number one (1). After responding to all the statements in each section, add each column up and record the total on the bottom row for each column.

Clinical Study Design

Knowledge, Skills and Abilities	Proficient	Able to Perform	Need Assistance to Perform
1. Develop a clinical study			
2. State purpose of a study			
3. Formulate a hypothesis			
4. Identify data elements required to test hypothesis			
5. Select best methodology for study			
6. Determine appropriate sample size			
7. Select appropriate statistical analysis methods			
TOTAL FOR EACH COLUMN			

Data Analysis

Knowledge, Skills and Abilities	Proficient	Able to Perform	Need Assistance to Perform
1. Differentiate between geometric mean and arithmetic mean			
2. Calculate a standard deviation			
3. Create a cumulative distribution chart for a data set			
4. Calculate the chi-square for a sample population			
5. Identify the type of data required to perform a correlation coefficient test			
6. Create a control chart			
TOTAL FOR EACH COLUMN			

Financial Analysis Skills

Knowledge, Skills and Abilities	Proficient	Able to Perform	Need Assistance to Perform
1. Differentiate the purpose of a balance sheet from a profit/loss sheet			
2. Identify the factors included in a cost-benefit analysis			
3. Calculate a return on investment			
4. Recognize factors to be excluded from cost-benefit analysis			
5. Identify centralized financial costs.			
6. Define a qualitative benefit			
TOTAL FOR EACH COLUMN			

Project Management

Knowledge	Proficient	Able to Perform	Need Assistance to Perform
1. Create a project plan			
2. Identify tasks and component parts			
3. Plan resource allocation			
4. Define critical pathway as used in a project			
5. Identify the four adjustments a project manager can make if a project is behind schedule.			
6. Describe how project milestones are spaced			
TOTAL FOR EACH COLUMN			

Data Management

Knowledge	Proficient	Able to Perform	Need Assistance to Perform
1. Use an automated spreadsheet to calculate a standard deviation			
2. Conduct a data base query			
3. Write specifications for information management needs			
4. Develop a presentation using at least one graphic package			
5. Produce a document which contains a table using a word-processing package			
6. Function in at least one operating environment			
TOTAL FOR EACH COLUMN			

Reengineering Principles

Knowledge, Skills and Abilities	Proficient	Able to Perform	Need Assistance to Perform
1. Develop a case for action argument			
2. Create a reengineering vision			
3. Differentiate between continuous quality improvement and re-engineering			
4. Differentiate between functions and processes			
5. Identify the five key players in reengineering efforts			
6. Identify common pitfalls of reengineering			
TOTAL FOR EACH COLUMN			

Miscellaneous Skills

Knowledge, Skills and Abilities	Proficient	Able to Perform	Need Assistance to Perform
1. Facilitate a behavioral change in a clinician			
2. Convert conflict into problem-solving in a group situation			
3. Diffuse an irate customer within five minutes			
4. Teach another staff member how to perform any task			
5. Facilitate a quality improvement team			
6. Write an action plan for correcting a JCAHO deficiency			
TOTAL FOR EACH COLUMN			

Overall Assessment

Directions: Copy the totals for each assessment section in appropriate spaces listed below. Add each column and record the total in the row designated for column total. Multiply this total by the number in the Multiple column and record the product in the last row. Add all point totals together and compare to key

Grand Total: _____

   Key 119-126=You're ready for the future
       105-118=You have great potential
       63-104=With a little work you'll be there
       42-62=Hard work can catch you up

What knowledge, skills and abilities are your greatest strengths?

What knowledge, skills and abilities are your biggest weaknesses?

2

Moving from a Quality Manager to a Performance Improvement Coordinator

With all the changes occurring within the health care industry, many questions arise regarding the necessary skills for the new performance improvement coordinators. This chapter focuses on the knowledge and skills required by quality improvement professionals to facilitate organizational performance improvement. Included in this skill set are:

1. Change management ability

2. Conflict management skills

3. Negotiation skills

4. Facilitation ability

Each of these skills and abilities will be explored in the following sections within the context of how to meet JCAHO standards for an integrated cross functional review process.

Change Management

Since the health care industry is in a constant state of fluctuation, the ability to plan and implement change in an organization is important for the performance improvement professional. This ability is especially important when a person does not have any formal authority over others. To serve as a change agent, certain knowledge, skills and abilities are required. The person must exhibit

- project management skills
- problem solving ability, and
- the ability to apply change theory to different situations

Each of these skills will be explored in the following sections.

Change Theory

Creating an environment to support change is the starting point for making planned changes. When the supporting structures and mechanisms are in place, there are a number of strategies that can be used to initiate the change process in a logical, consistent and measurable manner. This is especially true when making a large organizational change, such as moving from department-specific monitoring to a fully integrated cross-functional review process.

To create this environment, quality improvement professionals need to create a sense of direction, a sense of psychological safety and reinforce change attempts. **It is important to remember that people who have good self-esteem are generally willing to take risks and are more apt to change.**

Most of the current change modeling is based on the work of Kurt Lewin, who believed that change occurs in three basic steps: unfreezing, moving and refreezing. To unfreeze people, information sharing is essential to motivate the desire to change and to overcome resistance to change caused by fear and lack of information. Change information that should be shared includes:

- Description of the current situation
- Identification of deficits of the current situation
- Outline of how the change will occur.

Within the context of meeting JCAHO integrated review process standards, quality management professionals can communicate the following information.

In 1994, the Joint Commission revised their performance improvement standards to shift focus from department specific monitoring efforts to an organization-wide, coordinated cross-functional review effort. At the present time, we are still expecting the individual departments to conduct performance improvement monitoring independently. This situation has caused duplication of effort, lack of continuity of improvement efforts and small sporadic improvements throughout the organization. To help meet the new standards, reduce duplication and maximize efficiency of effort, we will be combining our current performance improvement efforts into performance improvement teams. These teams will be established by the Quality Council and the Medical Executive Committee and will focus on the main product lines provided by our organization. Department representatives will be assigned to the new teams based on the focus of their current review processes.

Once the unfreezing starts, performance improvement professionals need to address the emotional responses which follow. Confusion, discord, anxiety and hostility are frequently demonstrated when staff begins to recognize the need to change. During this phase, a performance improvement professional's role will change from teacher and prophet to facilitator and problem solver.

Next, steps are taken to move to the new paradigm. To promote this movement, the following questions need to be addressed:

- Is the direction clear and responsible?
- Does the change have a chance to succeed?
- Is the task framework specific rather than general?
- Is there an immediate outcome that can gratify and stimulate further action?
- Is the necessary power base established?

The answers to these questions impact the action strategies required to promote movement. Action strategies need to address:

- Personal–Meeting individual needs for power, prestige, growth and economics can enhance collaboration.
- Clout–Doing things at the right time for the right people ensures support for the change. Communication with people in power is essential. Upper management and medical staff support is instrumental for success.
- Negotiation–This is the key for implementing change and managing friction. Involvement breeds acceptance.

Each of your answer strategies needs to address the motivation and resistance forces which may keep people from moving to the new way of doing things. Besides using action strategies to promote change, performance improvement professionals need to plan the movement. The steps required to move others to the new situation will be explained in the project management section.

The final phase of change is refreezing. This phase consists of completing the intended change and validating the changed situation. Performance improvement professionals will frequently be responsible for collecting and analyzing data regarding the revised process and measuring the results of the change. Validating the change consists of collecting evidence that the environment reflects appropriate action, judgments reflect new values and past practices are not evident.

Some final thoughts on change are:

- Change is a process, not an event.
- Change could be easy if it were not for all "the people."
- People don't resist change, they just resist being changed.
- "There is nothing more difficult to take in hand, more perilous to conduct, more uncertain in its success, than to take the lead in the introduction of a new order of things"—Machiavelli, 1527.

Project Management

One of the key skills required by the new performance improvement coordinator is the ability to coordinate many projects focused on quality or resource improvement. This section discusses the foundational project management principles central to this ability.

Project Management Principles

To develop and manage a quality project effectively, quality professionals need to understand several principles of project management. These principles include:

- Implementation activities need to be divided into small tasks. Each task should be small enough that it can be accomplished within five working days. The ability to divide a large project into manageable tasks will increase the potential for success and prevent the feeling of being overwhelmed.
- The higher a person is in the organization's hierarchy, the longer the duration is between task assignments. For example, a staff nurse can be assigned a specific task every week while the unit director assignments should be every other week and so forth.
- Projects that fall behind can be put back on schedule through one of four methods: changing the timeframe, reducing the scope, assigning more resources or sacrificing quality.
- Tasks within a project need to be assigned to a specific person with the expertise to accomplish the task.
- Relationships between tasks need to be identified and assignments sequenced to ensure smooth implementation.
- Resources need to be identified to complete the assigned tasks. Resources include time, money, people, education and materials.
- Tasks should be linked to specific dates for completion.

By developing project management skills, performance improvement coordinators change from passive monitors to facilitators of change.

Project Activity	Start Date	End Date	Assignment	Resource
Implementing integrated performance improvement	1/1/95	3/30/95	QMC Coordinator	
A. Formulate the new structure for performance improvement	1/1/95	1/30/95	PI Coordinator	80 hours
A1. Formulate a structure for performance	1/1/95	1/5/95	PI Coordinator	23.75 hours
Write draft	1/2/95	1/2/95	PI Secretary	Forms tool 2 hours
Type draft	1/3/95	1/3/95	PI Secretary	8 hours
Approve draft	1/4/95	1/4/95	CQI Council	1 hour X 8 people
Retype survey	1/4/95	1/4/95	PI Secretary	1 hour Forms tool
Duplicate survey	1/5/95	1/5/95	PI Secretary	1 hour Copier
Write survey instructions	1/3/95	1/3/95	PI Coordinator	1 hour
Type survey instructions	1/3/95	1/3/95	PI Secretary	0.5 hour
Duplicate survey instructions	1/3/95	1/3/95	PI Secretary	0.25 hour Copier
Distribute survey instructions	1/5/95	1/5/95	PI Secretary	2 hours 25 internal mail envelopes

Problem Solving

You may have experienced problem solving as a one-step process—solve it. But there's more to it than proposing a solution and enforcing that decision. To effectively solve a problem or to lead others to solve their own problems, many evaluations, analysis and communication skills come into play.

In the following section, we will discuss a six-step problem solving model proposed by Richard Y. Chang and P. Keith Kelly. The steps, shown graphically below, involve defining the problem, analyzing potential causes, identifying possible solutions, selecting the best solution, developing an action plan and implementing the solution and evaluating progress.

Problem Solving Steps

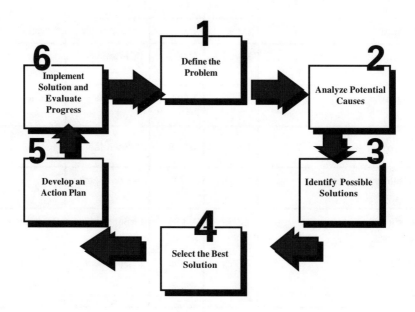

Define the Problem

The first step in effective problem solving is to define and clarify the problem being addressed. Even though this seems simple, it is extremely important to clearly define and agree upon the focus of problem solving efforts. Countless times problem solving has gone awry because people are busy solving the wrong problem or can not agree on what the problem is. The reason for this confusion is that people will frequently see a situation only from their own perspective.

To facilitate problem solving, performance improvement professionals need to ask themselves and others open ended questions such as:

- What is the current situation?
- What would the "desired state" look like if the problem were solved?

It is important during the problem definition step to avoid implying possible causes or suggesting solutions to the problem. Using our context of meeting JCAHO integrated review process standards, performance improvement professionals might state the problem like this:

> In 1994, the Joint Commission revised their performance improvement standards which focus on a department specific monitoring effort and an organization-wide coordinated cross-functional review effort. At the present time, we are still expecting the individual departments to conduct performance improvement monitoring independently. We need to consolidate these efforts into an organization-wide integrated review process.

Analyze Possible Causes

The second step in problem solving is to discover possible causes for a problem's existence. It is essential that performance improvement professionals guard against analyzing the symptoms of the problem instead of digging for the true root causes of the problem. "Cause and Effect Diagrams," also known as fishbone or Ishikawa diagrams, can help in identifying potential causes for a specific problem.

To develop a cause and effect diagram, brainstorm all the possible reasons why a problem exists. Then, group these into categories such as surroundings, systems, skills, suppliers, materials, methods, machines and people. Finally, lay out the identified reasons and groups as shown in the figure below. This Ishikawa diagram shows the possible reasons why there is currently departmental monitoring in our fictional institution instead of an organization-wide integrated review process.

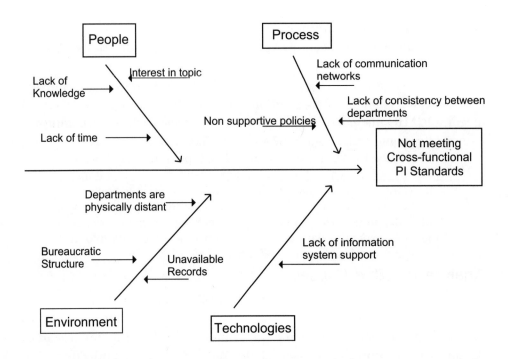

After identifying all possible causes for the problem, the most likely causes need to be identified. Performance improvement professionals can use a technique called Pareto analysis to determine the vital few causes from the significant many. Pareto analysis is based on the 80/20 rule (also called the Pareto Rule), which states that "80 percent of the wealth is held by 20 percent of the people." This rule can be restated to say 80 percent of the effect can be attributed to 20 percent of the causes.

To determine the vital 20 percent of a problem's causes, performance improvement professionals need to be able to construct a Pareto chart. The steps for constructing the chart are:

Step 1. Determine the categories and the units for comparison of the data.

Step 2. Total the raw data in each category, then determine the grand total by adding the totals of each category.

Step 3. Re-order the categories from largest to smallest.

Step 4. Determine the cumulative percent of each category, (the sum of each category plus all categories that precede it in the rank order, divided by the grand total and multiplied by 100).

Step 5. Draw and label the left-hand vertical axis with the unit of comparison.

Step 6. Draw and label the horizontal axis with the categories. List from left to right in rank order.

Step 7. Draw and label the right vertical axis from 0 to 100 percent. The 100 percent should line up with the grand total on the left-hand vertical axis.

Step 8. Beginning with the largest category, draw in bars for each category representing the total as measured on the left-hand axis.

Step 9. Draw a line graph beginning at the right-hand corner of the first bar to represent the cumulative percent of the total.

Step 10. Analyze the chart. A break-point in the cumulative percent line can indicate the vital few from the awkward zone and the useful many.

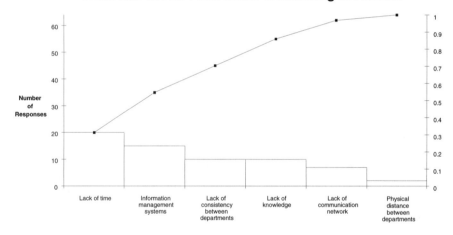

Reasons Cross-Functional Monitoring is Absent

Identify Possible Solutions

Once problem causes have been identified, it is time to generate ideas and alternatives for solving the problem. For most people, a natural reaction is to think about all the rules, regulations and what may be "politically correct." This kind of thinking restricts creativity when it comes to solving a problem. Sometimes, the most creative and unexpected approach to the problem brings the best results. Being creative means putting ideas on the table that might sound farfetched at first.

The goal of problem solving is finding the best solutions for the right cause. The first step in finding the "best solution" involves gener-

ating a list of possible solutions. In preparing this list, some simple guidelines should be followed:

- Avoid passing judgment or making comments on possible solutions. Sometimes this is done internally before a solution is even
  verbalized.
- Expand beyond your own experience and expertise. It is helpful
  to adopt the "walking in another man's moccasins" concept. Ask
  yourself, "What could I do if I were the CEO or the Chief of
  Staff?"
- Go for quantity. Try to come up with at least 20 possible solutions. This is especially important for very complex problems.

Once all the possible solutions have been generated, it is time to
determine the best solution. This can be done by debating the pros and
cons of each choice, taking a vote, using a decision matrix or using a paired
choice matrix.

A paired-choice matrix is a means to reduce the long list of *possible*
solutions to a short list of *most likely* solutions. This technique compares
each possible solution against the other possible solutions. To create a paired-
choice matrix, follow the steps outlined below.

Step 1. List all the possible solutions across the top row of a table.
Letter each choice starting with A.

Step 2. List all the possible solutions down the first column of a
table. Letter each choice with the same letter assigned in
step 1.

Step 3. Skip the comparison of solution A with itself and avoid the
other self-comparisons in the matrix.

Step 4. Compare choice A to choice B. Select the best solution between these two choices.

Step 5. Repeat step 4 with all the solution choices.

Step 6. Count up the number of time a particular solution was
selected as the best solution.

Step 7. Rank the solutions, in descending order based on the
frequency a solution was selected as the best solution.

For an example, let's use the paired-choice matrix to identify the
best possible solutions for meeting the Joint Commission's Performance
Improvement standard for an organization-wide review. A paired-choice
matrix appears on the following page analyzing the best solutions for in-
consistency between departments. The possible solutions being compared
are how to:

A. Educate managers on expectations

B. Implement standardized monitoring process
C. Centralize monitoring process and decentralize analysis process
D. Select new managers
E. Redesign organization along product lines

	A. Educate managers on expectations	B. Implement standardized monitoring process	C. Centralize monitoring process and decentralize analysis process	D. Select new managers	E. Redesign organization along product lines
A. Educate managers on expectations		B	C	A	E
B. Implement standardized monitoring process			C	B	B
C. Centralize monitoring process and decentralize analysis process				C	C
D. Select new managers					E
E. Redesign organization along product lines					

A Paired-Choice Matrix is used to select the best solutions for the organization's inability to meet the JCAHO organizational-wide performance improvement standards.

The raw results of this method are:
A. Educate managers on expectations = 1
B. Implement standardized monitoring process = 3
C. Centralize monitoring process and decentralize analysis process = 4
D. Select new managers = 0
E. Redesign organization along product lines = 2

Based on this technique, the two best solutions for meeting the Joint Commission's Cross-functional standards are implementing a standardized monitoring process and centralizing data collection and decentralizing analysis. These solutions address both the "lack of time" and the "lack of consistency between departments" causes of the defined problem.

Developing an Action Plan

At this point, the paper solution needs to be actualized through an action plan. The action plan outlines how the solution will be implemented, specifying what actions need to be taken, the timing of each action and who will perform the actions. The plan divides the solution into sequential, manageable tasks and activities. In other words, a project management plan will be developed and implemented.

Besides having a project management plan, performance professionals need to develop contingency plans. A contingency plan can be activated if the action plan gets waylaid or revised because of some event or change of circumstances. A contingency plan needs to address several key points:

- What specific opportunities and threats are likely to occur?
- What alterations are required to deal with identified opportunities and threats?
- What measures are required to prevent potential problems from arising?

While performance improvement professionals can't stop the unexpected from happening, they can plan for disruption by having a backup plan. With this plan available, the momentum gathered during implementation can be continued if these changes occur.

Keep in mind the rule of thumb: every minute spent planning saves 100 minutes of work and rework in the future.

Another method which is useful when creating contingency plans is to identify the force fields surrounding the identified problem and the desired solution.

Force field analysis is a technique used to identify the motivating forces for making a change and the restraining forces which block the change. To determine what these forces are, two questions need to be answered:

1. Why would people want to do this activity or solve this problem?

2. Why would people resist performing the activity or solving the problem?

By identifying the reasons for people's behavior, contingency plans can be developed to address these underlying reasons rather than addressing only observable behaviors.

Implementing Solutions and Evaluating Progress

The step that closes the problem solving loop is the solution implementation and the evaluation of the action plan's effectiveness. Although circumstances, priorities and people change over time and sometimes solving a particular problem gets lost within the chaos of day-to-day life, it is important to complete this step in the process. Successful efforts involve:

- Collecting data according to the action plan
- Implementing contingency plans when necessary
- Evaluating results and identifying new problems created by the solution

Performance improvement professionals can use the action plan as a data collection questionnaire to determine if the project is on track. If the project is varying from the plan then a contingency plan is needed to move the process toward the "desired state."

Evaluating the results and identifying new problems created by the solution is the final activity in the problem solving process. The loop is completed by assessing whether the desired outcome has been accomplished and if the required infrastructure is present to prevent the recurrence of the identified problem.

Conflict Management Skills

Besides being change agents, quality improvement professionals must be able to manage conflict between individuals and groups. This involves recognizing conflict, understanding the causes of conflict and implementing conflict management techniques to diffuse and resolve existing conflict.

Conflict can wear many faces and can be evidenced by rejection, avoidance or open hostility. The next table shows several conflict statements.

Type of Conflict	Individual Behavior	Group Behavior
Rejection	"I don't have time to do anyone else's work." Passive-aggressive behavior	Continuing to do present monitors
Avoidance	Missing meetings Not returning phone calls Quitting	Not sharing available information at department meetings
Hostility	Loudly refusing to change Making threats	Blaming others for not cooperating Job Actions

Understand Causes of Resistance

To effectively deal with resistance and to defuse conflict, performance improvement professionals need to understand the causes of conflict. Most conflicts arise over differences in facts, methods, roles, resources, goals and/or values. The true reasons for a particular conflict can be discovered by asking open-ended, impersonal questions.

Strategies for Managing Conflict

To manage conflict effectively, the following principles should be applied to the conflict situation:

- *Listen, listen, listen.* This will allow you to discover the true reason, instead of the assumed reason, for the conflict.
- *Ask open-ended questions.* The agenda for the conflict is in the question. Allow others to ask you only three questions in a row before you ask a question. More than three consecutive questions turns a conflict into an interrogation.
- *Focus on the reason for the conflict.* Work toward defining the cause of the conflict. This will allow you to convert the conflict into problem solving.
- *Remember the rule of interdependency.* The conflict will end, but

the relationship must continue. As soon as possible, reestablish the relationship.

- *Avoid dilemmas by giving more than two choices.* This prevents a win-lose situation.
- *Decelerate the conflict to the lowest level possible.* The lower the conflict level, the easier to negotiate a resolution.

Seven Levels of Conflict

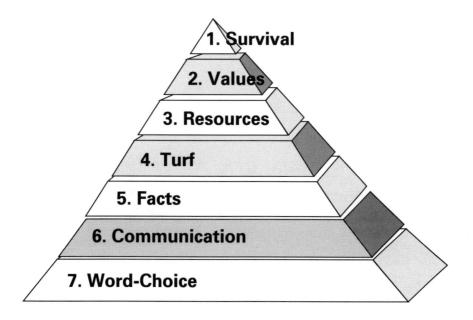

1. Survival
2. Values
3. Resources
4. Turf
5. Facts
6. Communication
7. Word-Choice

Negotiation Skills

Whenever people are asked to change, negotiation may come into play. Negotiation promotes acceptance of change which may be in conflict with past experience, special interests, values or beliefs.

It does not matter whether a performance improvement professional is called upon to negotiate a managed care contract or ratification of a developed pathway, the principles are the same:

- Listen for what the other person really wants or what is keeping the person stuck where he or she is.
- Break big issues into sub-issues. This will allow both sides to give and take.
- Do your homework. Know the facts and the position taken by the other side.
- Know your limits and do not violate those limits. Crossing this line is a surrender, not a negotiation.
- Be willing to walk away from the table.

Besides knowing the principles of negotiation, there are some guidelines for conducting negotiation:

1. Identify the issues.

2. Provide an opportunity for people to express themselves without challenge or debate.

3. Clarify the differences and points of agreement after each speaker.

4. Acknowledge and accept points of agreement.

5. Identify options for converting conflicts to areas of agreement.

6. Continue the process until a consensus is reached.

If an impasse is reached after attempting to negotiate consensus then the topic needs to be set aside until additional information is available.

By becoming proficient with orchestrating change, managing projects, solving problems, managing conflict and negotiating, a performance improvement professional has the necessary skill set to facilitate teamwork among caregivers and health care departments.

3

Moving to Integrated Systems of Care

Although quality assurance/improvement, utilization review, infection control and risk management all have responsibilities of monitoring the quality, efficiency and safety of patient care and related services, these tasks are frequently found in separate departments or services. Because of this fragmentation, quality management professionals frequently have to review the same patient's information several times. By segregating review functions according to *tasks* the potential for duplications and inefficiencies are increased.

During the past ten years, health care organizations have embraced the concept of continuous quality improvement. Continuous quality improvement can be defined as a process for making incremental improvements within the framework of existing processes. Frequently these efforts were established as a separate function from the traditional patient care review activities This decision established an environment of competition and alienation among existing quality and resource monitoring processes.

This chapter deals with using critical pathways as the means of integrating patient care review and continuous quality improvement activities. ***Critical pathways provide a mechanism for integrating continuous quality improvement (CQI) efforts with traditional patient care review activities and do not constitute an additional process***. By the end of this chapter each reader can expect to:

1. Describe how pathways integrate patient care review activities

2. Discuss the principles of developing and implementing pathways

3. Explain the steps in developing a pathway

4. Assess an organization's readiness for developing and implementing pathways

Common Characteristics of All Improvement Processes

To start the process of integration, the quality management professional must first recognize the common elements and principles which are present in all quality, resource and safety improvement processes. Based on these common elements, processes can be developed to meet the purpose and requirements of all functions.

Category of Characteristics	Utilization Review	Quality Assessment & Improvement	Continuous Quality Improvement	Risk Management	Infection Control	Discharge Planning
Case Finding	Yes	Yes	Yes	Yes	Yes	Yes
Process Review	SI & IS	Clinical	Clinical & Administrative	During Investigation	Outbreak Investigation	
Outcome Measurement	L.O.S.	Clinical Outcomes	Process Outcomes & Satisfaction	Sentinel Event Rates	Infection Rates	Placement
Variance Investigation	Outliers	Peer Review	Common Cause	Incidents Investigation	Nosocomial Investigation	
Data Analysis	Yes	Yes	Yes	Yes	Yes	
Peer Review	Yes	Yes				
Team Concepts	Yes	Cross Dept.	Yes			Yes
Timing of Review	Concurrent	Concurrent or Retrospective	Concurrent or Retrospective	Concurrent Retrospective	Concurrent	Concurrent

Clinical Continuous Quality Improvement

Because quality, resource and safety initiatives use common processes for case finding, process monitoring, outcome measurement and data analysis, there need to be monitoring, analysis and communication systems which support an organization's decision-making ability. One of the fundamental mechanisms which can accomplish this integration is the development and implementation of critical pathways. Pathways address many of the functions which are present in current patient care review activities and continuous quality improvement efforts. Therefore, pathways are an extension of these review processes.

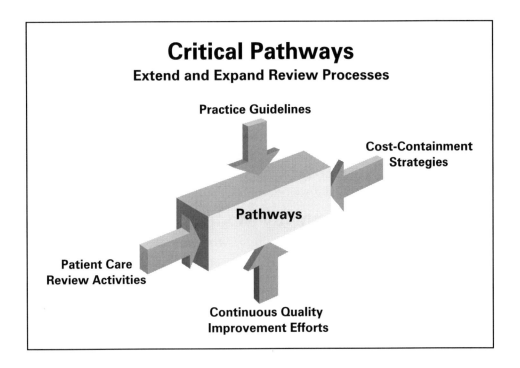

Critical Pathways
Extend and Expand Review Processes

Practice Guidelines

Cost-Containment Strategies

Pathways

Patient Care Review Activities

Continuous Quality Improvement Efforts

What Are Pathways?

Pathways are a mechanism for transforming a reactive bureaucratic ritual into a dynamic, indispensable clinical improvement process. Once the key players "buy-in" to the process, pathways become a mechanism for:

1. Integrating CQI with traditional patient care review

2. Proactively addressing economic and regulatory changes

3. Improving clinical outcomes through reduction in variations

4. Controlling unnecessary costs and resource usage

5. Fostering a multi-disciplinary approach to patient care

6. Linking quality management to staff education

Common Characteristics

Despite differences in terminology, perceptions and scope, most critical pathway efforts share certain characteristics. These common features are found throughout the health care industry, regardless of where the pathway is developed or used.

- All critical pathways are designed for a specific patient population.

- Pathways are the result of careful consideration and consensus-building among caregivers.
- Critical pathways focus on the nature, amount, timing, sequence or duration of patient care activities. Pathways can include elements related to clinical assessments, procedures, medications, treatments, consultations, diagnostic studies, discharge planning, patient education and follow-up care.
- Critical pathways identify desired patient outcomes.
- Pathways are validated systematically through data analysis over time, facilitating continuous improvement of the pathway.

The QTA Critical Pathway Model

One method for developing your own pathways which will address the unique characteristics of your patients and organization is a five step process initiated by Quality Team Associates in 1991. This approach integrates the scientific process with change theory, problem solving and project management. A summary of the five-step process is presented below.

Steps in Developing and Implementing Pathways

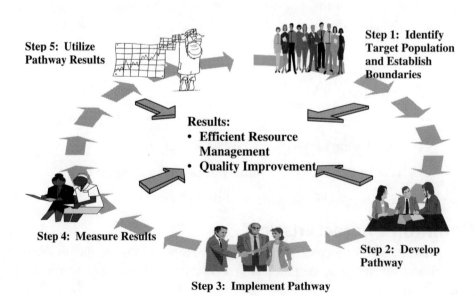

Step 5: Utilize Pathway Results

Step 1: Identify Target Population and Establish Boundaries

Results:
• Efficient Resource Management
• Quality Improvement

Step 4: Measure Results

Step 2: Develop Pathway

Step 3: Implement Pathway

Identification of Target Population and Pathway Boundaries

The first step identifies populations that will benefit the most from a critical pathway and establishes the scope of the pathway. This process involves four key components:

1. Develop selection criteria
2. Review available data
3. Select a patient population for the pathway
4. Establish pathway boundaries

Identification of Target Population and Pathway Boundaries

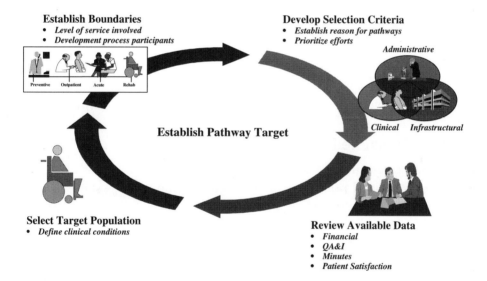

Establish Boundaries
- *Level of service involved*
- *Development process participants*

Preventive   Outpatient   Acute   Rehab

Develop Selection Criteria
- *Establish reason for pathways*
- *Prioritize efforts*

Administrative

Clinical   Infrastructural

Establish Pathway Target

Select Target Population
- *Define clinical conditions*

Review Available Data
- *Financial*
- *QA&I*
- *Minutes*
- *Patient Satisfaction*

Selecting Target Population

At the start of the development process, an oversight group needs to evaluate the entire patient population to identify potential patient groups for pathway development and to establish organizational priorities for developing these pathways. To accomplish this evaluation, selection criteria are needed to provide an objective basis for decision-making. Selection criteria will address administrative, clinical and infrastructural reasons for selecting specific patient groups.

Administrative Selection Criteria

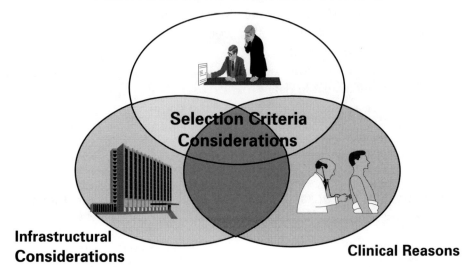

Clinicians can develop and use any number of selection criteria, although it's recommended they choose the five to seven most important factors.

Review Available Data

Once selection criteria have been established, clinicians can identify and prioritize target populations. The identification process starts by applying selection criteria to available health care data.

Most health care organizations use a variety of data sources to communicate and document patient care processes and outcomes, administrative issues and staff activities. These sources assist clinicians with identifying populations and processes for critical pathways. Among the most productive information sources are:

- Financial reports
- Patient care review information
- Comparison data base information
- Committee and department minutes and reports
- Patient, community and staff surveys

Diagnosis	199? Adm.	Our Avg. LOS	Nat'l Avg. LOS	Org. Avg. Chg.	Avg. Nat'l Pmt.	Annual Loss
Chronic Obstructive Pulmonary Disease	36	7	5.8	$4000	$3100	-$32,400
Simple Pneumonia and Pleurisy with Co-morbidities	34	7	7	$4500	$3600	-$30,600
Circulatory Disorders with AMI and Cardiovascular Complication, Discharged Alive	15	8	7.8	$5600	$5000	-$9,000
Circulatory Disorders with AMI Expired	5	30	2.9	$4000	$4400	+$2000
Heart Failure and Shock	38	8.0	6.0	$4000	$3100	-$34,200
Angina Pectoris	16	3.0	3.6	$1500	$1900	+$6,400
Chest Pain	10	3.0	2.7	$1500	$1600	+$1000
Total/Partial Hip Replacement	25	7.6	6.2	$10000	$6800	-$80,500
Total Reimbursement	179					-$176,800

Review available data to determine where the organization can benefit the most from critical pathways.

Select the Patient Population

At this point, the oversight committee will, using its professional judgment, apply the selection criteria developed earlier to the population data gathered in the previous section. This process will render the target population for the pathway.

A suggested approach for performing this analysis is to develop a decision matrix. A decision matrix promotes team work and consensus among practitioners by enabling them to discuss different perspectives and information en route to selecting a patient population. ***Keep in mind, however, that the committee makes the decision, not the decision matrix.***

Decision Matrix for Selecting Patient Populations

Patient Care Topic	High Vol.	Easy to Implement (Wt. X 2)	Fin. Loss	Varia-nces	New Guide -lines	Total	Rank
Pneumonia	6	1 (2)	4	3	2	17	5
CHF	5	2 (4)	2	6	6	23	3
Hip Fracture	4	4 (8)	5	4	3	24	2
C-Section	1	6 (12)	1	1	5	20	4
COPD	3	3 (6)	3	2	1	15	6
Total Hips	2	5 (10)	6	5	4	27	1

A decision matrix enables clinicians to prioritize pathway development efforts using objective data and group consensus.

Establish Critical Pathway Boundaries

Now that a target population has been selected, **pathway boundaries** must be established. The boundaries define the points of service where a pathway starts and ends. **The scope of the pathway includes the range of services available between these two points**.

Scheduled Total Hip Replacement Boundaries Can Include a Variety of Health Care Settings

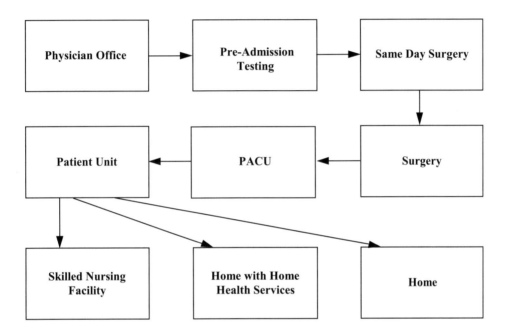

Since critical pathways can be developed for any points of service along the continuum of care, clinicians need to decide which points will be addressed in the pathway. ***A pathway can be developed in stages or as a complete process*** depending on the resources available and the degree of "buy-in."

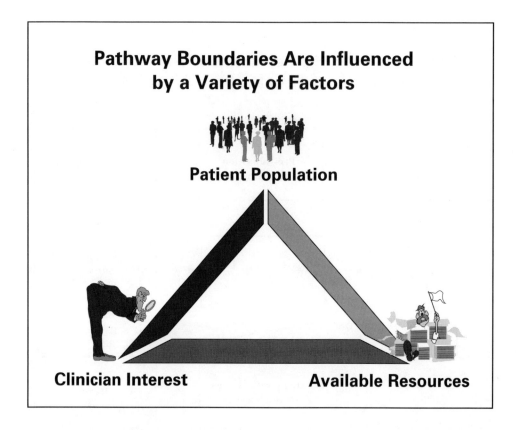

There are two models which can be used when establishing pathway boundaries. One is a medical model which will meet the needs of clinicians in acute care and home health settings. The other model is a functional model which meets the needs of long-term care, rehabilitation, psychiatric and long-term home health patients.

The medical model focuses on a specific diagnosis, procedure or medication, while the functional model deals with the functional level of the target population.

Building the Pathway Blocks

Timing Intervals of Treatment Based on Functional Level

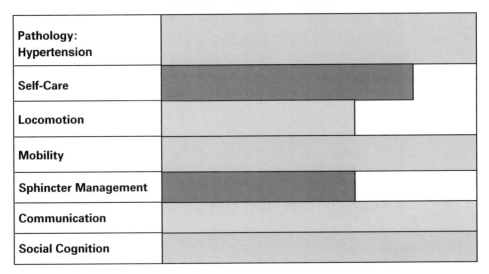

	0-72 hrs	Level I	Level 2	Level 3	Level 4
Pathology: Hypertension					
Self-Care					
Locomotion					
Mobility					
Sphincter Management					
Communication					
Social Cognition					

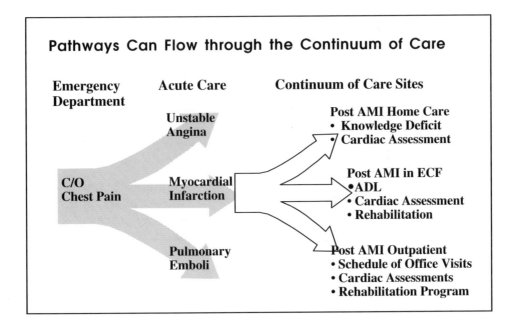

Pathways Can Flow through the Continuum of Care

Emergency Department

Acute Care

Continuum of Care Sites

Unstable Angina

C/O Chest Pain

Myocardial Infarction

Pulmonary Emboli

Post AMI Home Care
• Knowledge Deficit
• Cardiac Assessment

Post AMI in ECF
• ADL
• Cardiac Assessment
• Rehabilitation

Post AMI Outpatient
• Schedule of Office Visits
• Cardiac Assessments
• Rehabilitation Program

Formulating a Team

Once a patient population has been selected and pathway boundaries defined, a pathway development team needs to be formed. This team can be an established committee, such as the Special Care Committee, or a newly created continuous quality improvement team.

The pathway development team should be multidisciplinary, must have physician involvement and needs to include staff members involved with the day-to-day care of the target patient population. Clinical services, such as pharmacy, laboratory and radiology, who provide support to the direct caregivers, should serve as consultants to the team when their clinical expertise is required.

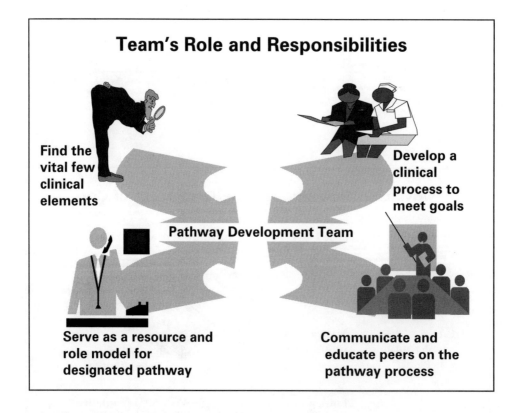

Team's Role and Responsibilities

Find the vital few clinical elements

Develop a clinical process to meet goals

Pathway Development Team

Serve as a resource and role model for designated pathway

Communicate and educate peers on the pathway process

Development of Pathway

The second step in the QTA Critical Pathway Model follows the development of a critical pathway through identification of "best practice" and standardization of current processes. This step consists of seven components, which are discussed in the following section.

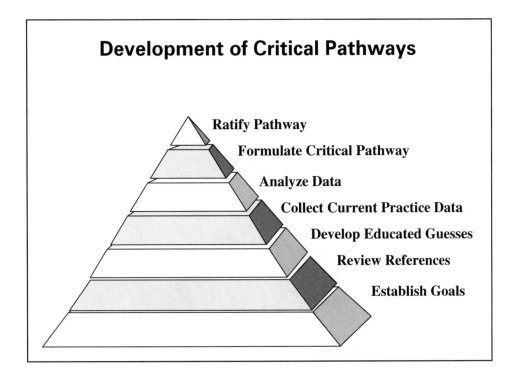

Development of Critical Pathways

- Ratify Pathway
- Formulate Critical Pathway
- Analyze Data
- Collect Current Practice Data
- Develop Educated Guesses
- Review References
- Establish Goals

Establish Pathway Goals

Critical pathway goals provide a measuring stick for the effectiveness of the pathway. Most pathway goals measure patient outcomes, efficiency of the system, cost of care or customer satisfaction.

To start developing these goals, clinicians should review previously stated criteria for selecting the patient population. Goals that emerge from this review need to be consistent with the reasons for targeting this group for pathway development.

When developing goals, consideration needs to be given to the "Dimensions of Quality" outlined in the Joint Commission for Accreditation for Healthcare Organization (JCAHO) Standards. Quality dimensions include **efficacy, appropriateness, availability, timeliness, effectiveness, continuity, safety, efficiency of services and respect and caring for patients.** By establishing pathways goals which focus on these areas, clinicians can measure both the efficiency and quality of care.

Another factor influencing pathway goal development is the scope of the pathway. Goals relate directly to the clinical processes found within the pathway boundaries.

Review External References

The analysis of external references provides a foundation for developing hypotheses and identifying potential elements in a pathway. By collecting and reviewing information from various outside sources, clinicians can:

- Identify the practice parameters for safe care
- Formulate data collection questions based on available research and commonly accepted "standards of practice"
- Identify regulations and guidelines mandating minimum requirements
- Discover other critical pathways to use as models

After clinicians have collected and analyzed the available data, they are ready to develop and test hypotheses about what elements are critical for high quality and efficient care.

Develop Hypotheses

To proceed with developing a critical pathway, clinicians need to develop educated guesses or assumptions about how to obtain the desired pathway goals. These hypotheses are based on the information gleaned from external references combined with past clinical experience.

A hypothesis states a clinician's belief about the relationship between specific patient care activities and patient outcomes. Forming hypotheses is important because it provides the logic for consensus building, directs information requirements and guides the selection of analytical tools. Hypotheses will be related to the timing, duration, content of assessments and interventions. Hypotheses state the causal relationship between an intervention and the desired patient or financial outcome.

Pathway Development
Systolic Dysfunction Congestive Heart Failure

- The avg. length of stay will be reduced to 5 days.
- **The nosocomial pulmonary edema rate will be reduced to 2%.**
- The readmission rate for the first 30 days post-discharge will be reduced to 3%.

Pathway Goals
- Quality
- Safety
- Resources

Pathway Hypotheses
- Application of practice guidelines, experience, professional judgment
- Links clinical process with patient outcomes
- Basis of critical thinking and clinical decision making

- The type of DIURETIC impacts the P.E. rate.
- The initial timing of DIURETIC THERAPY impacts the P.E. rate.
- The type of DIET impacts the P.E. rate.
- The frequency of BREATH SOUNDS ASSESSMENT impacts the P.E. rate.
- The ordering of CALCIUM CHANNEL BLOCKERS increases the P.E. rate.
- The ordering of ACE INHIBITORS impacts the P.E. rate.

There are some general guidelines for writing pathway hypotheses. These guidelines include:

Guidelines	Examples
Focus on one pathway goal at a time, to help focus the development effort.	All interventions which will impact the respiratory failure rate.
Select interventions which will impact the attainment of the goal	Anticoagulants, chest X-rays, how to use tri-flow bottles, etc.
State the type of measurement for the designated intervention	Frequency, timing, number, content, sequence, duration, presence, etc.
Identify how the intervention will impact the designated patient outcome.	Increase, decrease, correlate, impact, reduce.
Use neutral terms to state each hypothesis	The type of diuretic will impact the length of stay for patients with CHF.

After hypotheses are developed and agreed upon for each pathway goal, clinicians are ready to develop data collection questions and collect relevant information.

Pathway Goal for Scheduled Congestive Heart Failure	Hypotheses about how to meet established goals
Average length of stay will be five days	The timing of discharge planning impacts the length of stay

The timing of diuretic therapy being initiated impacts the length of stay.

The timing of vasodilator administration impacts the length of stay.

The use of oxygen therapy impacts the length of stay.

The type of pain management impacts the length of stay.

The assessment of breath sounds impacts the length of stay. |

Collection of Current Practice Data

Hypotheses must be tested with current practice data. In the testing process, relevant data is collected, organized and analyzed, enabling clinicians to accept or reject hypotheses and to formulate critical pathways.

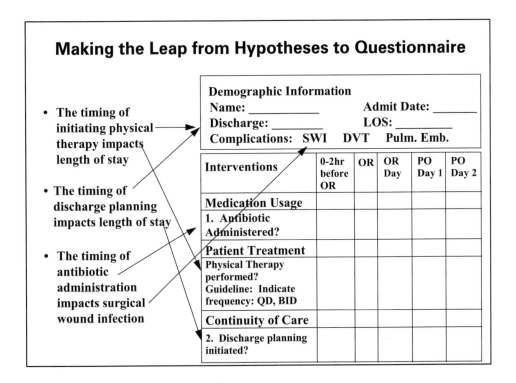

After clinicians agree on the data required to test the hypotheses, a mechanism to capture this information must be developed. This mechanism can be manual, semi-automated or automated. Regardless of the method, issues related to question development, case selction guidelines, questionnaire directions, sampling methodology and data collection methodology must be addressed.

The information extracted during the pathway development process can be used to meet monitoring and evaluation requirements, such as drug usage evaluation, pertinence of medical records, surgical case reviews and interdisciplinary reviews.

Collection of Current Practice Data

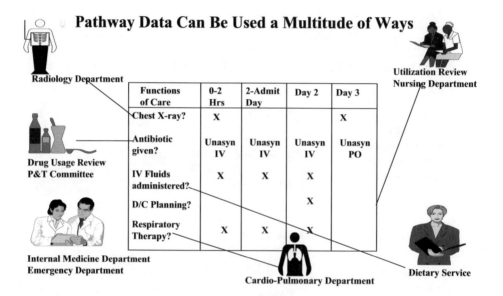

Pathway Data Can Be Used a Multitude of Ways

Radiology Department

Drug Usage Review
P&T Committee

Internal Medicine Department
Emergency Department

Utilization Review
Nursing Department

Dietary Service

Cardio-Pulmonary Department

Functions of Care	0-2 Hrs	2-Admit Day	Day 2	Day 3
Chest X-ray?	X			X
Antibiotic given?	Unasyn IV	Unasyn IV	Unasyn IV	Unasyn PO
IV Fluids administered?	X	X	X	
D/C Planning?			X	
Respiratory Therapy?	X	X	X	

Analyze Current Practice Data

Before clinicians can develop and ratify a critical pathway, the collected data must be systematically analyzed. This analysis provides objective evidence of the relationship between certain diagnostic or treatment interventions and patient outcomes. Clinicians integrate this evidence with collective experience, professional judgment and common sense to select critical pathway elements.

To perform data analysis, clinicians must select appropriate statistical tests, plan the presentation of collected data and test the established hypotheses.

The type of analysis depends on sample size and the relationship among data elements being tested. Generally, critical pathway hypotheses address a causal relationship between clinical interventions and patient outcomes, or a comparison among different interventions. To confirm or reject the stated hypothesis or belief, the appropriate statistical tests are applied and the results discussed.

Organizing Raw Data into Patterns of Care
is the First Step to Analysis

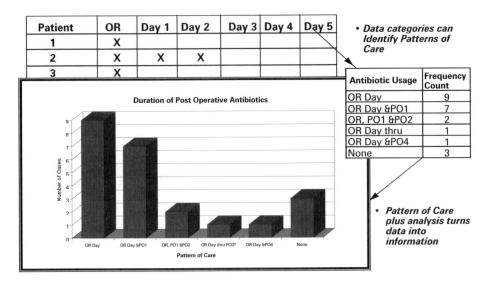

Patient	OR	Day 1	Day 2	Day 3	Day 4	Day 5
1	X					
2	X	X	X			
3	X					

• Data categories can Identify Patterns of Care

Antibiotic Usage	Frequency Count
OR Day	9
OR Day &PO1	7
OR, PO1 &PO2	2
OR Day thru	1
OR Day &PO4	1
None	3

• Pattern of Care plus analysis turns data into information

The first step in selecting appropriate analysis techniques is to re-view the stated hypotheses and identify the relationships being tested. This testing of hypotheses enables clinicians to link process to outcomes and converts chart review to data management.

Descriptive Analysis

Hypothesis: The timing of physical therapy impacts the length of stay.

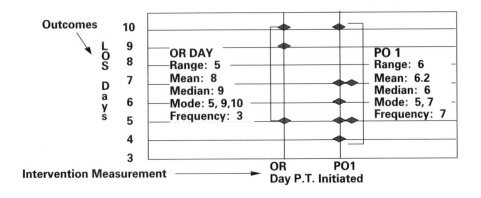

The second step in selecting an appropriate analysis technique is to determine if the sample size is sufficient for performing the desired test. Many tests either have minimum sample size requirements or vary in their degree of confidence based on the size of the group.

Inferential Analysis: Scattergram

Hypothesis: The timing of physical therapy impacts the length of stay.

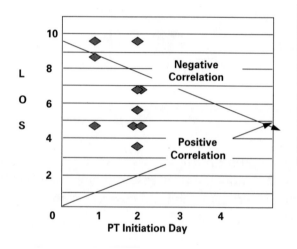

Day of P.T.	LOS (Days)
2	4
1	9
2	5
2	5
1	10
2	7
1	5
2	6
2	7
2	10

Correlation Coefficient: - 0.376
Colton Rule: Fair Degree

Each hypothesis will be accepted or rejected based on the clinicians' analysis of data. ***Thus, the critical pathway will be built by incorporating care activities accepted as being supportive of the desired outcomes***, while the care activities categorized as being contrary or non-contributing to the pathway goals will *probably* be excluded.

Formulate a Critical Pathway

At the completion of data analysis, clinicians are ready to create the critical pathway. ***The pathway will include specific clinical assessments and interventions and will designate the timing for these activities***. The inclusion of each element in the pathway is negotiable.

Formulate a Pathway

Timing of Interventions

Pathway Functions	0-2 Hrs	2 Hours thru Admit Day	Day 2
Patient Assessment	Breath sounds TPR & B/P	TPR &B/P q8h Dyspnea level Breath sounds	TPR &B/P q8h Dyspnea level Breath sounds
Diagnostic Studies	Chest X-ray CBC Blood Cultures Pulse Oximetry or ABG		
Medication Usage	IV Unasyn 1.5 gm	IV Unasyn 1.5 gn q6h Non-narcotic analgesic prn	IV Unasyn 1.5 gn q6h Non-narcotic analgesic prn
Patient Treatment	IV started O_2 per 4l if Sat <94%	IV 1000 cc q8h O_2 per 4l if Sat <94%	IV 1000 cc q8h O_2 per 4l if Sat <94%
Patient Education			Medication Ed. Food interactions with antibiotics
Continuity of Care		Discharge Planning	
Patient Outcomes			Dyspnea level improves 1 level

Functions of Care

Ratify a Critical Pathway

After a pathway has been developed, it needs to be submitted for ratification by the clinical staff. Ratification gives approval and/or formal sanctioning to the pathway. How this is accomplished will depend on an organization's structure, the disciplines involved and the purpose of the pathway.

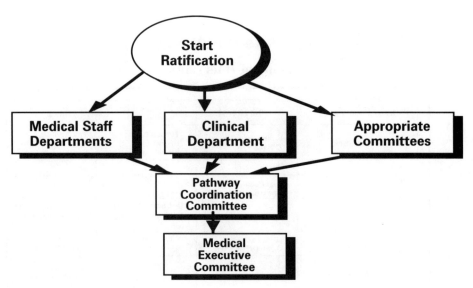

Ratification processes are influenced by the medical staff by-laws, the organization's sanction process and the intended use of the developed pathway.

Implementation of Critical Pathways

Once a critical pathway has been developed, it is actualized through the implementation process. The implementation process is a strategy to ensure acceptance of the pathway and to facilitate modifications of clinical practice.

Implementation of Critical Pathways

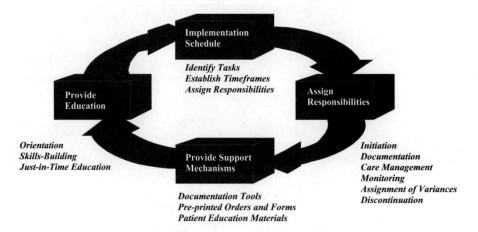

During the implementation phase, organizations determine how critical pathways will fit with current patient care delivery and review processes. They must assess whether or not the current infrastructure can support critical pathways.

Establish an Implementation Schedule

To begin the implementation process, clinicians need to create a schedule of tasks for "rolling out" the developed critical pathways. *This schedule will designate required activities and establish a timeline for those activities*

Clinicians need to decide what implementation activities are appropriate for the pathway and organization. Once the implementation activities have been agreed upon, they need to be broken into sub-components of workable size. Scheduling of activities is influenced by the level of expertise and resources required, the relationships between tasks and the mapping of the tasks to specific calendar dates.

Assign Responsibilities

To effectively implement and maintain critical pathways, organizations need to assign specific roles and responsibilities to staff members. The four basic sets of responsibilities for implementing and maintaining critical pathways are:

Assignment of Responsibilities

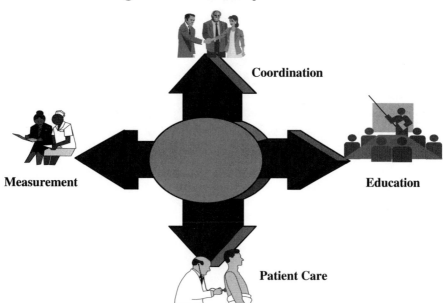

Coordination

Measurement

Education

Patient Care

Each of these responsibilities can be assigned to either an individual or a group to ensure the desired change in patient outcomes.

Development of Support Mechanisms

Support mechanisms need to be established to ensure consistent and accurate use of the developed critical pathways. These support mechanisms can provide guidance, reduce documentation time and facilitate effective case management. The type of supportive mechanisms required for successful implementation may include:

1. Medical record forms

2. Implementation guidelines

3. Patient education materials

Effective support materials will facilitate pathway compliance without limiting a practitioner's right to make decisions.

Medical Record Forms

One major concern of clinicians is related to increasing paperwork. To address this, consideration needs to be given to streamlining and standardizing patient care documentation without sacrificing quality and pertinence of medical records.

The medical record forms that support critical pathway compliance include:

- Pre-printed physician orders
- Standardized progress notes and flow sheets
- Pre-written referral forms
- Patient education materials and documentation forms
- Multi-discipline treatment plans or nursing kardexes
- Electronic laboratory and radiology test panels

These are the basic mechanisms for communicating information between clinical disciplines and recording vital patient information. Documentation systems for supporting pathways should be built on mechanisms already in place for communicating clinical assessments and interventions.

Creating a Documentation System

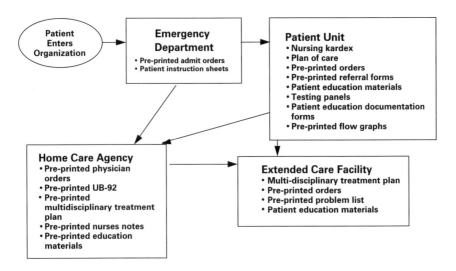

It is important that clinicians record only patient-centered information and *not* practitioner or system variances in the medical record.

Implementation Guidelines

Implementation guidelines communicate staff responsibilities, define key terms and outline pathway procedures. These guidelines can take the form of instruction sheets or organizational policies and procedures. Pathway guidelines need to clearly communicate **staff responsibilities, definition of key terms and pathway procedures.**

Probably the most important part of critical pathway guidelines is the outline of critical pathway procedures. These procedures describe the steps required to implement, use and document a critical pathway. Once critical pathway guidelines are developed, they can form the basis for critical pathway orientation and just-in-time education.

Critical Pathway Clinical Process

Patient Education Materials

Patient education conveys two types of information. First, patients must be given information about self-care activities, such as proper transfer techniques, insulin administration and how to do dressing changes. Secondly, patients must be made aware of the critical pathway, the expectations for their role in the pathway process and the expected patient outcomes. By acquiring this information, patients are able to:

1. Collaborate with caregivers to actively participate in their own care

2. Understand and reach expected patient goals

3. Make preparations for post-pathway care

Provision of Staff Education

One of the key ingredients for a successful critical pathway implementation is to provide appropriate, timely and relevant staff education. There are three basic types of education associated with implementing critical pathways.

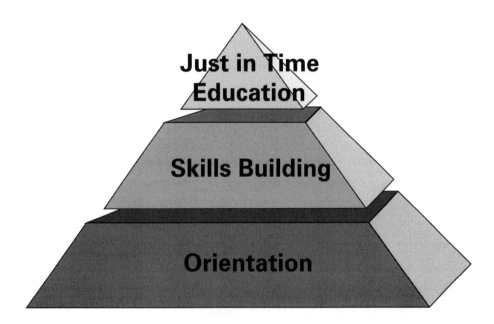

Measurement of Results

After a critical pathway has been implemented, the impact on patient care needs to be measured. This is done to *assess pathway compliance, discover opportunities for improvement* and *evaluate goal attainment*. Clinicians must establish a monitoring system which addresses the collection and analysis of pathway information.

Assignment of Responsibilities

We have designated the term ***care coordinator*** to refer to the individual assigned the task of managing a patient's care according to a specific critical pathway. The term is synonymous with ***clinical case manager***.

Under this definition, the care management function is limited to managing the clinical aspects of patient care. The role does *not* encompass the financial aspects of the case.

The range of responsibilities for a care coordinator includes:

1. Facilitating utilization of pathways
2. Documenting the care provided
3. Initiating actions to correct pathway deviations

The individual assigned the task of overseeing individual pathways, coordinating discharge planning and conducting utilization review activities is called a ***case coordinator*** or ***resource case manager***.

Identification of Pathway Data

The final issue in developing a monitoring process involves which critical pathway information should be collected for analysis. It is advisable for organizations to collect information about individual pathway elements, the reasons for variance from the pathway and the outcomes of the pathway.

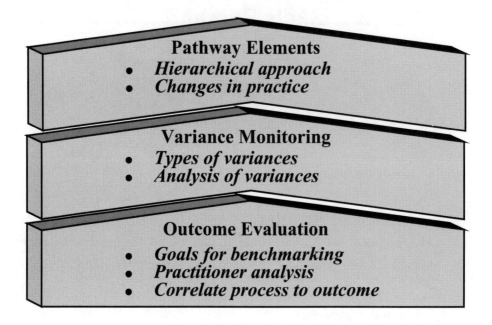

Pathway Elements
- *Hierarchical approach*
- *Changes in practice*

Variance Monitoring
- *Types of variances*
- *Analysis of variances*

Outcome Evaluation
- *Goals for benchmarking*
- *Practitioner analysis*
- *Correlate process to outcome*

Measuring Pathway Elements

Since clinicians are monitoring a critical pathway and not a clinical pathway, all elements are essential and should be monitored. By monitoring the presence or absence of each scheduled pathway intervention, an organization can:

- Assess the stability of the patient care process
- Make refinements to the existing critical pathway
- Validate established pathway elements
- Refine existing pathways

To truly validate the developed pathways, quality professionals need to collect data on cases which are on pathways and cases which qualify but are not on a pathway.

Measuring Reasons for Variance

The second type of measurement relates to identifying the reasons for pathway variations. By investigating the reason for pathway deviations, areas for improvement can be identified and evidence can be accumulated to support new or existing continuous quality improvement efforts. The reasons for pathway deviation can be grouped into three categories:

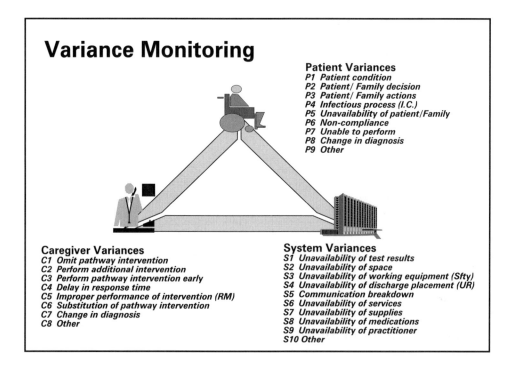

Variance Monitoring

Patient Variances
P1 *Patient condition*
P2 *Patient/ Family decision*
P3 *Patient/ Family actions*
P4 *Infectious process (I.C.)*
P5 *Unavailability of patient/Family*
P6 *Non-compliance*
P7 *Unable to perform*
P8 *Change in diagnosis*
P9 *Other*

Caregiver Variances
C1 *Omit pathway intervention*
C2 *Perform additional intervention*
C3 *Perform pathway intervention early*
C4 *Delay in response time*
C5 *Improper performance of intervention (RM)*
C6 *Substitution of pathway intervention*
C7 *Change in diagnosis*
C8 *Other*

System Variances
S1 *Unavailability of test results*
S2 *Unavailability of space*
S3 *Unavailability of working equipment (Sfty)*
S4 *Unavailability of discharge placement (UR)*
S5 *Communication breakdown*
S6 *Unavailability of services*
S7 *Unavailability of supplies*
S8 *Unavailability of medications*
S9 *Unavailability of practitioner*
S10 *Other*

Those monitoring care need to remember to rule out system and patient variances prior to identifying a variance as a practitioner issue. The reason for this sequence is that critical pathways only address the critical elements of care. Additional elements may be required to provide optimal care because of the patient's condition or the need to work around system inadequacies.

Decision Model for Assigning Variances

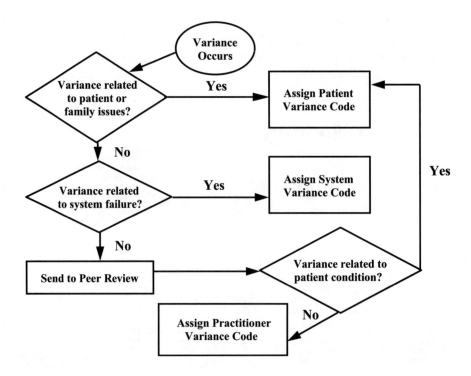

Measuring Patient Outcomes

Monitoring patient outcomes is the last type of critical pathway measurement. Outcome measurements can focus on the attainment of daily progress goals (if they were developed) and/or individual case outcomes. By aggregating the individual case outcomes, clinicians can measure the degree to which a critical pathway meets its intended purpose and validates the relationship between clinical processes and outcomes.

Critical Pathway Monitoring Process

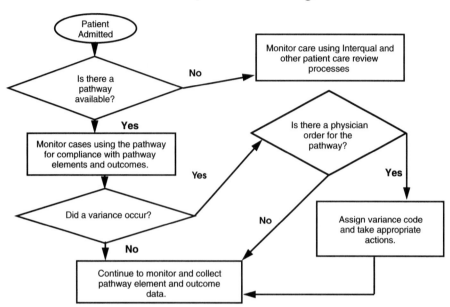

Case Management Plans

To efficiently and consistently collect pathway measurement data and to manage patients on pathways, clinicians should develop a case management plan. This document serves as a pathway monitoring form and collects valuable data which can be used for performance improvement purposes.

The case management plan contains information about critical pathway activities, the actions taken to promote pathway compliance and the reasons for deviations from the pathway. Additional information, such as discharge planning and insurance review information, may be recorded on the case management form if it lies within the case manager's responsibilities.

To ensure consistent use of the case management plan, explicit instructions need to be developed for both the management process and for filling out the form.

Outcome Measurements:

1. Disch. Day 5 or less	☐ Yes	☐ No
2. Readmit w/i 30 days	☐ Yes	☐ No
3. Acute respiratory failure	☐ Yes	☐ No

Adm Date: _____ Disch Date: _____
LOS: _____ Nursing Unit: _____
Diagnosis:
Procedure:

Addressograph Stamp

Aspects of Care	0-2 hours	Day 1	Day 2	Day 3	Day 4	Day 5
1. Assessments	1. Dyspnea level 2. Breath sounds 3. Skin color 4. T, P, R & B/P 5. LOC	1. Dyspnea level tid 2. Breath sounds q4h 3. Skin color tid 4. T, P, R & B/P q4h 5. LOC q4h	1. Dyspnea level tid 2. Breath sounds q4h 3. Skin color tid 4. T, P, R & B/P q4h 5. LOC q4h	1. Dyspnea level tid 2. Breath sounds q4h 3. Skin color tid 4. T, P, R & B/P q4h 5. LOC q4h	1. Dyspnea level tid 2. Breath sounds qid 3. Skin color tid 4. T, P, R & B/P qid 5. LOC qid	1. Dyspnea level 2. Breath sounds 3. Skin color 4. T, P, R & B/P
2. Diagnostic Tests	1. Chest-X-ray 2. ABG 4. ECG 5. Electrolytes 6. Sputum for Gram Stain if purulent 7. Pulmonary function 8. Theophylline Serum level if on theophylline	2. ABG	2. ABG	2. ABG	7. Pulmonary function test	
3. Medications	1. Beta Agonists 2. Steroids 3. Antibiotic if purulent sputum	1. Beta Agonists 2. Steroids 3. Antibiotic if purulent sputum	1. Beta Agonists 2. Steroids 3. Antibiotic if purulent sputum	1. Beta Agonists 2. Steroids 3. Antibiotic if purulent sputum	1. Beta Agonists 3. Antibiotic if purulent sputum 4. Anticholinergics	1. Beta Agonists 3. Antibiotic if purulent sputum 4. Anticholinergics
4. Treatments	1. Oxygen at 1-2l per nasal cannula 2. Respiratory therapy	1. Oxygen at 1-2l per nasal cannula (if Po_2 below 55) 2. Respiratory therapy	1. Oxygen at 1-2l per nasal cannula (if Po_2 below 55) 2. Respiratory therapy	1. Oxygen at 1-2l per nasal cannula (if Po_2 below 55)	1. Oxygen at 1-2l per nasal cannula (if Po_2 below 55)	1. Oxygen at 1-2l per nasal cannula (if Po_2 below 55)
6. Nutrition/Fluids	1. Start IV	1. IV with D_5W	1. IV with D_5W	1. IV with D_5W	1. D/C IV	
7. Activity	1. Head of bed elevated	1. Head of bed elevated	1. Head of bed elevated 2. Up in chair	1. Head of bed elevated 2. Up in chair 3. Pulmonary rehab	1. Head of bed elevated 2. Up in chair 3. Pulmonary rehab	1. Head of bed elevated 2. Up in chair 3. Pulmonary rehab
8. Patient Education	1. Purse-lipped breathing	2. Effective coughing techniques 3. Treatment expectations	4. Medication education 5. Disease process	4. Medication education 6. Activity restriction 7. Smoking cessation	8. Percussion techniques and postural drainage	4. Medication education 6. Activity restrictions 7. Smoking cessation
9. Continuity of Care	1. Admit to ICU	1. ICU	1. Transfer to Medicine 2. Discharge planning	2. Refer to homecare 3. Arrange home oxygen if patient will use at home	2. Homecare admission assessment	
10. Outcomes					1. Discharge if discharge criteria met	1. Discharge if discharge criteria met

Resource Case Manager Data Sheet

Patient Outcomes:

Demographic Information	
Admit Date: _____	D/C Date: _____
Pathway: _____	
Working Diganosis: _____	
Procedures: _____	

LOS:
Complications: _____
Other: _____

Addressograph Imprint

☐ No variance noted in the case   ☐ Patient not on pathway

Patient Codes	System Codes	Practitioner Codes	Action Codes
P1: Patient condition	S1: Availability of test results	C1: Omit pathway intervention	A1: Request additional information
P2: Patient/Family decision	S2: Availability of space	C2: Perform additional intervention	A2: Request change in orders
P3: Patient/Family availability	S3: Availability of working equipment (Sfty)	C3: Perform pathway intervention early	A3: Provide staff education
P4: Patient/ Family actions	S4: Availability of discharge placement	C4: Delay in response time	A4: Obtain functioning equipment
P5: Patient/ Family ability to perform activity	S5: Communication breakdown	C5: Improper performance of intervention (RM)	A5: Contact another practitioner
P6: Non-compliance	S6: Availability of services	C6: Substitution of pathway intervention	A6: Reschedule intervention
P7: Change in diagnosis	S7: Availability of supplies	C7: Change in diagnosis	A7: Discontinue pathway
P8: Infectious process (IC)	S8: Availability of medications	C8: Other	A8: No action taken
P9: Other	S9: Availability of practitioner		A9: Other
	S10: Other		

Case Management Action Plan:

Instructions: Record the date of each variance from the pathway, the pathway element number, the variance code, corresponding actions, any additional comments and your initials in the appropriate space listed below. If no variances are noted in the case, check the box below **patient outcomes.**

Date	Function of Care	Pathway Element	Timing of Var.	Var. Code	Action Code	Comments	Reviewer's Initials

Return completed form to the Quality Management Department within 24 hours of patient discharge.

Analysis of Data

Once data has been collected for the established critical pathway, it needs to be analyzed so that continuous quality improvement occurs.

Clinicians frequently wonder what to do with critical pathway data. This information can be aggregated to:

1. Identify process and outcome variations
2. Provide insights into health care system breakdowns
3. Compare actual practice with formulated goals

To accomplish critical pathway analysis, comparisons must be made among pathway elements, clinicians' performance, reasons for variations and patient outcomes.

Pathway Elements

First, the proportion of cases complying with each critical pathway element needs to be analyzed to determine the stability of the developed process. This analysis can be done longitudinally to show changes in the critical pathway process over time and to validate the appropriateness of the established pathway.

Individual critical pathway elements can be analyzed to determine where deviations occur most frequently along the pathway. Determining where variances occur in the pathway helps focus investigation on reasons for the variance.

Analyzing critical pathway elements can help practitioners to determine the presence or absence of deviations. However, this analysis does not explain why deviations occur or how deviations affect the outcome of the case. To understand either of these aspects, clinicians need to incorporate information about variation issues and outcome data.

Pneumonia Chest X-Rays Compliance

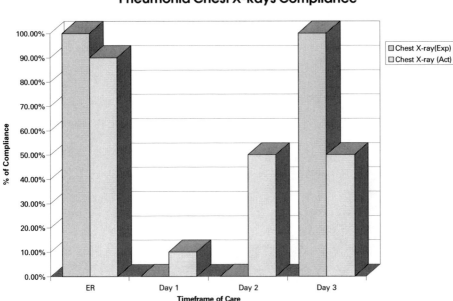

Reasons for Variance

Once a deviation from a critical pathway is found, the reason for this variance needs to be investigated by the care manager. The reasons for variances are then aggregated and analyzed:

1. To identify opportunities for improvements
2. To assist with targeting future pathway populations

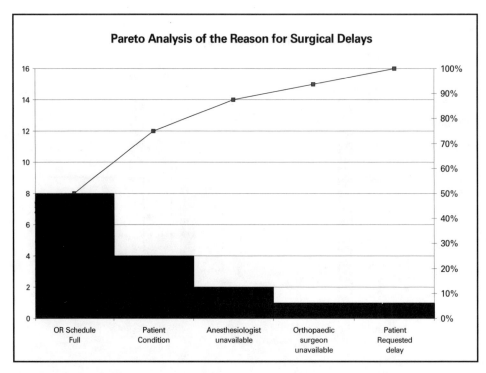

Pareto Analysis of the Reason for Surgical Delays

Pareto analysis charts are a cumulative frequency distribution method for identifying the vital few reasons for variance.

Patient Outcomes

The final type of analysis concerns outcome measurements, which evaluate:

- The attainment of established pathway goals
- Comparisons between cases that complied with, to cases which deviated from, the pathway
- Correlations between critical pathway elements and patient outcomes

In addition to these three main outcome analyses, clinicians may wish to compare outcomes to those found in outside data sources.

Outcome Measurement

Evaluating attainment of all goals

» **Demonstrates impact of pathway**

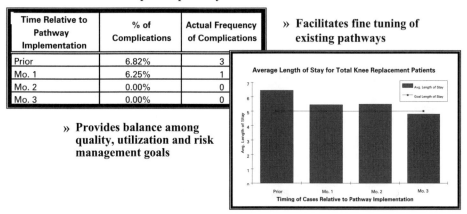

Time Relative to Pathway Implementation	% of Complications	Actual Frequency of Complications
Prior	6.82%	3
Mo. 1	6.25%	1
Mo. 2	0.00%	0
Mo. 3	0.00%	0

» **Facilitates fine tuning of existing pathways**

Average Length of Stay for Total Knee Replacement Patients

» **Provides balance among quality, utilization and risk management goals**

Utilization of Critical Pathway Results

The final step in the QTA Five Step Critical Pathway Process, utilization of pathway results, focuses on managing critical pathways through a changing health care environment, population shifts and the emergence of new technologies and practice guidelines. By effectively using pathway results, quality professionals can sustain the improvement realized during pathway implementation, demonstrate the accomplishment of stated goals and foster "buy-in" for future critical pathway projects.

Utilization of Pathway Results

- **Reinforcement of Desired Performance**
- **Identification of Triggers**
- **Implementation of Pathway Revisions**

Implement Revisions

- *Activate Revision Process*
- *Initiate Implementation Process*
- *Measure Impact*
- *Formalize Revision*

Reinforce Performance

- *Reward System*
- *Feedback*
- *Removal of Impediments*

Identification of Triggers

- *Practitioner*
- *Institutional*
- *Community*

Reinforcement of Desired Performance

Clinicians can promote pathway compliance and remove impediments to desired results by effectively using the critical pathway data previously collected and analyzed. ***Attainment of desired results can be encouraged by providing positive reinforcement and relevant feedback to practitioners and eliminating pathway impediments***. A consistent positive reinforcement system increases the probability that desired behaviors will become the new "standards of practice."

Feedback of pathway results informs clinicians about how they are meeting established expectations and assists them in planning future pathway-related activities. Based on their awareness of pathway results, individual clinicians can adjust their practice, compare their performance to group norms and initiate education to improve their knowledge, skills and abilities.

The final area for reinforcing desired performance deals with the removal of impediments to critical pathways. These impediments can include:

1. Non-supportive policies and procedures
2. Absence of necessary equipment, space, services or staff
3. Insufficient knowledge, skills or abilities to perform the re-

quired actions

By using critical pathway variance data, clinicians can spot the major causes of pathway variances and take measures to eliminate them.

Identification of Triggers

Triggers are conditions or events that precipitate an evaluation and/or revision of the current critical pathway. For an event to qualify as a trigger, it must have a *sustained impact* on the health care environment. Special events are not triggers.

The three main categories of pathway triggers are:

1. **Practitioner**: Events or conditions which alter practitioners' compliance with established pathway.
2. **Institutional**: Conditions or events occurring within an organization that impact the services available to customers.
3. **Community**: Conditions or events that impact the population served by a healthcare organization.

Implementing Pathway Revisions

Critical pathway revision requires a systematic mechanism incorporating many of the same activities found in the development and implementation steps in the overall critical pathway process. The revision process integrates these activities with an organization's CQI process.

By continuously measuring critical pathway results and utilizing this information to reinforce and revise desired performance, clinicians can keep their pathways relevant, usable and "state of the art." Also, by incorporating involved clinicians' professional judgments and collective experience with new guidelines and technologies, *critical pathways become a living guide for care and not an established "cookbook."*

Assessing Organizational Readiness for Pathways

When an organization contemplates developing and implementing pathways, many concerns arise regarding required resources and how pathways will impact the organization.

Organizational Requirements

Prior to introducing pathways, an organization should conduct a self-assessment to provide necessary information to its decision-makers. This assessment should evaluate the presence of the basic organizational requirements for successful pathways. The seven requirements are:

1. Upper Management Commitment
2. Medical Staff Involvement
3. Clinician Support
4. Existence of Organizational Performance Improvement Processes
5. Good Communication Networks
6. Good Data Management Mechanisms
7. Adequate Time

These elements need to be present or pathways will be between difficult and impossible to initiate and maintain. A sample pathway assessment questionnaire is provided at the end of this chapter.

Upper Management Commitment

Although each organizational requirement listed above should be present to achieve successful pathway implementation, the most fundamental prerequisite is upper management commitment. You may be wondering why upper management commitment is so vital to pathway success, especially since pathways are considered clinical processes. Simply put, the development, implementation and utilization of pathways frequently require a paradigm shift in an organization.

The new paradigm moves the organization from an isolated and department specific patient care approach to a collaborative and multi-disciplinary patient management system. To accomplish this change, upper management needs to establish expectations for the pathway process and create or change existing organizational infrastructure to meet those expectations.

The key tasks for upper management in supporting pathways are to define and assign key responsibilities, to formulate a process for pathway development and implementation and to provide resources in support of clinicians' pathway efforts.

Assignment of Responsibilities

Three of the most important responsibilities required to support the development of a pathway process are the oversight function, the pathway coordination function and the case coordination function. The oversight function ensures consistency in the pathway development and implementation process. The coordination function provides day-to-day management of the organization's pathway process. Case coordination facilitates pathway compliance and consistent evaluation of pathway variances.

An oversight committee provides a central clearinghouse for all pathway efforts, thus reducing the risk of duplication of efforts, ensuring priority selection of appropriate patient populations and facilitating a consistent process for developing pathways and communicating pathway information. Without this oversight and coordination function, pathways can spring from all areas of the organization using different development methodologies. As a result, there is a risk of inconsistent pathway quality and duplication of efforts.

Oversight responsibility can be given to an individual, an established committee, such as the Quality Management Committee or Quality Council, or to a new group, such as a Pathway Steering Committee. Regardless of who is assigned responsibility for overseeing the pathway process, they must have decision-making authority to change the organization's infrastructure to meet pathway requirements. A suggested constituency for a pathway oversight committee includes:

- Medical staff leaders
- Vice-presidents of operations, clinical services and finance
- Representatives from medical records, information management services, quality management, utilization review and staff development

The responsibilities assigned to the oversight group include:

1. Providing overall critical pathway process direction
2. Coordinating critical pathway implementation efforts

3. Developing an effective structure for implementing and revising critical pathways
4. Facilitating critical pathway communication and education
5. Collaborating with involved clinicians to evaluate pathway effectiveness

Day-to-day coordination of the organization's pathway process can be assigned to an existing position or to a newly created position. Regardless of who is assigned responsibility for it, the coordination function facilities pathway activities and enables consistent execution of decisions made by the oversight committee.

Coordination responsibilities include:
1. Serving as an internal consultant for pathway development and implementation processes.
2. Facilitating critical pathway team efforts through problem solving, mediation and negotiation.
3. Providing pathway orientation and education to new employees, medical staff members and pathway team members.
4. Fostering communication among pathway teams, involved clinicians, appropriate committees and administrators.

The final key assignment of responsibilities concerns who will be the case coordinators for those patients on critical pathways. There is no consistent pattern throughout the health care industry for designating case coordinators.

Case coordination responsibilities include:
1. Monitoring for appropriate application of and compliance with developed pathways
2. Documenting variances along with the reasons for variances
3. Taking appropriate measures to facilitate future pathway compliance
4. Providing staff education regarding pathway interventions

By assigning responsibilities for these key functions and delegating sufficient authority to the selected positions and groups, upper management provides essential leadership in support of critical pathways.

Establish Pathway Processes

The second key responsibility for upper management is to establish the structure for developing and implementing pathways. This structure needs to outline the procedures for developing, communicating, implementing and utilizing pathways, thereby promoting consistent pathway quality and providing needed direction to pathway teams. To determine the processes required for consistent and coordinated pathway development, upper management needs to answer the following questions:

1. How will pathway topics be selected?
2. What steps will each pathway development group need to accomplish to create a relevant and useful pathway?
3. How frequently should pathway groups communicate with clinical departments and committees?
4. What information should be shared about pathways throughout the organization?
5. What format will be used for pathways at this organization?
6. What is the implementation process for pathways?
7. How will pathways be monitored and results used after a pathway is completed?

Provide Resources for Pathway Efforts

And as a final effort, upper management must provide the necessary resources to support the pathways. These resources include financing, sufficient clinician time for pathway development and implementation, availability of financial and clinical information, so pathway decisions are based on information rather than opinion, and sufficient people with the necessary skills to develop and implement pathways successfully.

By providing the necessary leadership, structure and resources, upper management can build a solid foundation for an organization's pathway efforts, greatly increasing the chances for success. This support empowers clinicians in making the necessary changes to the health care delivery system for maximizing pathway compliance and developing realistic, relevant pathways.

Medical Staff Involvement

The next key prerequisite for successful pathway efforts is the support and involvement of the medical staff. Medical staff support is imperative for pathways because the primary therapeutic relationship in health care is between a physician and his or her patient. If the medical staff does not support pathway efforts, those efforts are doomed to have a limited impact on improving patient care outcomes.

Pathway processes are greatly enhanced by the knowledge, abilities and skills that physicians possess. As the scientists in the organization, they have the ability to lead teams in developing scientifically sound pathways.

How can organizations convince medical staff members to participate in the pathway process, particularly since most physicians already donate their time to support medical staff activities at the health care facility? The best way is to demonstrate the benefits which will result from pathway development.

Physician benefits from pathways include:

- ***Pathways reduce the "hassle factor" for routine orders and care.***
- ***Pathways facilitate rapid documentation of orders, progress notes, and consultation forms.***
- ***Pathways help in attaining managed care contracts.***
- ***Pathways encourage consistent high quality care for patients***
- ***Pathways provide a mechanism for improving practice standards.***

Clinician Support

Besides having both upper management and medical staff endorsements, critical pathways also need to be **supported by all involved clinicians**. This support is important because of the cross-functional, multidisciplinary nature of pathways. Without widespread support and collaboration, pathways will be used inconsistently throughout the organization and will fail to meet the desired goals for the process.

- **Clinicians need to participate in the development, implementation and use of pathways.** Without this involvement, critical pathways will become a paperwork exercise without tangible benefits.
- At the outset, **clinicians can support the pathway effort by sharing their expertise in the development phase**. This expertise will become the cornerstone for pathway content and problem solving regarding how to handle specific patient care problems.
- **Clinicians need to consistently follow the policies and procedures outlined to develop, implement, use and document pathways.** By following these procedures, inefficiencies and shortcomings in the process can be identified and corrected.
- **The last key area for clinician support is identification of potential targets for pathway development and/or revision.** This contribution will help pathways promote improved care and reduced costs for the organization rather than provide an exercise to appease one of the "paper gods" of health care.

Existence of Organizational Performance Improvement Processes

Once support of key medical, administrative and clinical staff has been generated, attention needs to be directed toward establishing an infrastructure for the pathway process. This infrastructure should be built on concepts and processes used by existing performance improvement activities. By using existing infrastructure, pathways can be easily integrated into current patient care review and quality improvement activities instead of being an additional process the organization needs to support.

By combining the basic structural aspects from quality assessment, utilization review and continuous quality improvement to form the foundation for pathway infrastructure, performance improvement activities can be streamlined and integrated into a coordinated, organization-wide process.

Communication Systems

One of the key ingredients for pathway success is an open communication system. This is essential because pathways are built on teamwork and require information to be freely communicated for evaluation, coordination and decision-making. Pathway effectiveness is greatly reduced by communication restrictions.

Several of the basic issues that impact communication within an organization is the trust between disciplines and departments and the organizational stress on collaboration versus competition. Often, the creation of an environment of cooperation requires an organization to undergo a paradigm shift from competition for recognition to cooperation in decision making.

Pathway Data Can Be Used a Multitude of Ways

Total / Partial Hip Replacement Data

Treatment Modalities	OR Day	Day 2	Day 3	Day 4
Antibiotic given?	X	X		
Anticoagulant given?		X	X	X
Disch. Planning		X		
Phys. Therapy started?		X		
Solid food initiated?		X		
Pain Management?	PCA	PCA	PCA	IM/PO

Basis of Inventory

Basis of Physician Orders

Identification of Staff Requirements

Basis of Multi-disciplinary Patient Care Review

Basis of Communication and Documentation

Useful for Contract Negotiations

Support of Reengineering Efforts

Answers to the following questions can be used to determine the best means for communicating pathway data and information :

1. What mechanisms are currently used to communicate new policies and procedures?
2. How are suggestions communicated to management regarding changes or improvements to current processes?
3. How does communication occur between departments when there is a problem?
4. Is cross-department communication encouraged or does it require permission from a supervisor in order to occur?
5. What mechanisms are currently available to a group or department for obtaining data from another department in the organization?

Information Management Systems

Because the development, implementation and monitoring of critical pathways is extremely data intensive, provisions for managing clinical and financial data are crucial. In most organizations, that infrastructure is based on a strategic information management plan, which should be consulted prior to initiating pathways.

Existing information management mechanisms should have the capability of supporting pathway data collection and analysis requirements with relatively minor changes. If the current information management infrastructure can't support collection and analysis of pathway data, pathway processes will be labor intensive and very difficult to implement successfully.

Pathway data management requires staff with data analysis expertise and some degree of computer hardware and software support. This ability is required to identify current "Patterns of Care" and to correlate their patterns with the resulting outcomes. To accomplish this, additional skills may be required beyond medical records abstraction and analysis.

Information presentation mechanisms are significant for giving both clinicians and administrators a uniform view of pathway information. These mechanisms, however, do not have to be well developed to begin pathway activity.

Access to Current Information

Access to information about current practice, practice guidelines and outcome measurements is vital during pathway development. This information will enable clinicians to establish realistic outcome measurements and to identify current standards and regulations that can impact the developed pathways.

Time

The last requirement for successful pathway process is time. **Critical pathways are not quick fixes for chronic problems.** Rather, they provide a means for developing long-term ("continuous and never-ending") improvement. Because pathways frequently change the way an organization does business, it takes time to develop and implement new or expanded policies and procedures, revise or restructure existing organizational systems, train staff and develop effective pathways.

Administrators and medical staff leaders need to establish a strategic critical pathway plan with realistic timeframes when embarking on pathway development. This plan needs to allocate enough time to assess organizational readiness for pathways, develop the necessary infrastructure and develop and implement pathways.

Once the supporting infrastructure has been put in place, an organization is ready to produce its first pathway. It must be emphasized that pathway development takes time. If sufficient time is not provided, then short cuts are taken and the result may be a pathway that does not improve outcomes or lower costs or is expensive to monitor.

Without sufficient support, infrastructure and time, pathways can squander an organization's time and resources. This waste will manifest itself as duplication of effort, unmanageable data, inappropriate pathways, unused pathways and power struggles.

Unmet Pathway Requirements Can Land an Organization in Dangerous Waters!

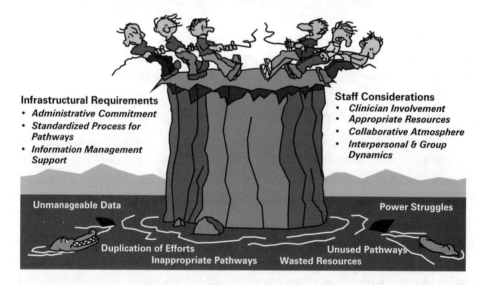

Infrastructural Requirements
- *Administrative Commitment*
- *Standardized Process for Pathways*
- *Information Management Support*

Staff Considerations
- *Clinician Involvement*
- *Appropriate Resources*
- *Collaborative Atmosphere*
- *Interpersonal & Group Dynamics*

Unmanageable Data

Power Struggles

Duplication of Efforts
Inappropriate Pathways

Unused Pathways
Wasted Resources

Exercise: Determining Pathway Readiness

Step 1. Using the category stated in the first column, list your organization's possible issues which will prohibit or limit pathway success. Record these issues in the second column.

Step 2. As a group, share these issues and develop a plan for addressing these identified issues and record these in the third column.

Pathway Requirement	Identified Issues Which will Impede Pathway Process	Proposed Plan for Addressing Issues
Upper Management Support		
Medical Staff Involvement		
Clinician Support		

Pathway Requirement	Identified Issues Which Will Impede Pathway Process	Proposed Plan for Addressing Issues
Organizational Performance Improvement Foundation		
Communication System		
Information Management Systems		
Time		

4

Strategic Planning for Reengineering Quality in an Organization

Introduction

With recent changes in the Joint Commission's accreditation standards, there is increasing impetus to integrate services according to functions of care or morbidity types. This movement promotes organizational restructuring efforts to integrate existing departments and services into **Patient Focused Care Units.** Patient focused care is a delivery model based on a cross-functional approach to providing care according to identified product lines, such as cardiovascular, orthopedics or women's services. This approach differs from the traditional delivery system which emphasizes discipline specific or service departments such as pharmacy, social services and nursing.

Health Care Systems Need to Reengineer Current Processes

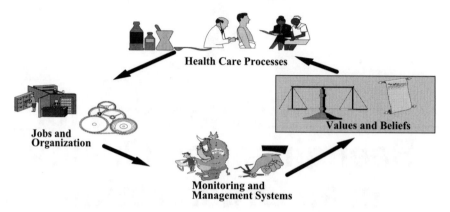

What is the impact on the quality improvement, discharge planning, infection control, utilization review and risk management departments when an organization moves to providing cross-functional care? The most obvious result is the need to integrate current patient care review activities into a coordinated monitoring and analysis system. This integration will merge existing departments, redefine job responsibilities, revise monitoring processes and increase data management demands.

This chapter focuses on how to reengineer the existing patient care review processes to meet the changing organizational needs by focusing on the following:

- Explaining reengineering principles
- Identifying the differences between reengineering and continuous quality improvement
- Describing how to reengineer existing patient care review departments
- Developing a strategic plan to meet future quality and resource needs

Reengineering

One of the new buzz words being used by health care executives and others is the term **reengineering**. Reengineering, according to Michael Hammer and James Champy, is "the fundamental rethinking and radical redesign of processes to achieve dramatic improvements in critical, contem-

porary measures of performance, such as cost, quality, service and speed."
Secondly, reengineering is not synonymous with downsizing, automation,
restructuring, delayering or total quality management. Reengineering focuses on **what must be done** and then **how to do it**. This change is brought
about through radical redesign of essential processes which result in dramatic improvements.

Reengineering differs from total quality management in several ways.
While quality programs work within the current framework of the organization to make incremental improvements to existing processes, reengineering
seeks to reinvent the organization and replace processes. The goal of total
quality improvement is to do current processes better. **The goal of
reengineering is to invent new approaches to essential health care
processes**.

Although reengineering differs from total quality management, there
are several similarities. Both processes recognize the importance of process
and work backwards from the needs of the process to the customers.

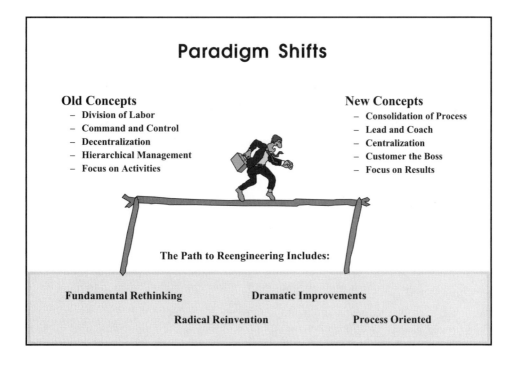

Reengineering Principles

Before exploring how to reengineer current monitoring processes a basic understanding of reengineering principles must be obtained. This understanding begins with the knowledge of some basic reengineering principles.

- Fundamental processes are reengineered, not departments.
- Reengineering occurs from the top down.
- Several tasks are combined into one process.
- Work needs to be performed when it makes the most sense.
- Work needs to be performed where it makes the most sense.
- Processes have multiple versions .

Each of these basic principles will be explained further in following sections.

Focus on Redesigning Processes

The first reengineering principle is focus on fundamental processes and not on a department or other organizational unit. By focusing on processes, jobs, people and organizational structures, dramatic changes can be accomplished. For example, if an organization focuses on reengineering the quality management department, then only incremental improvements can be made because the quality management department is responsible for only part of the monitoring process. However, if an organization focuses on reengineering the patient care monitoring process then dramatic changes will be realized by all departments and services that conduct patient care monitoring.

Focus Reengineering on Fundamental Processes

Current Process

- Discipline Specific
- Administrative Task Specific

Reengineered Process

- Providing Treatment
- Obtaining Payment
- Obtaining Accreditation

Identify Fundamental Processes

- What must be done?
- Why do we do what we do at all?

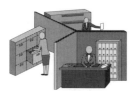

Functional departments fragment processes

Processes have a beginning and an end

Reengineer from the Top Down

Reengineering can never happen without top management support. There are two reasons for this axiom. One is that middle management and front-line employees lack the broad perspective that reengineering demands. The second is reengineering inevitably will cross organizational boundaries and require upper management authority to make changes.

To accomplish reengineering, there needs to be a senior executive leader who can act as visionary and motivator. This leader is self-nominated and self-appointed rather than assigned the responsibility. The reason for this is it is difficult to mandate a person to have a vision. The reengineering leader must:

- Articulate a vision of the "new" organization and standards
- Induce others to translate the vision into reality
- Create an environment conducive to reengineering
- Inspire others with a sense of purpose and mission

The reengineering leader can demonstrate leadership through signals, symbols and systems. Signals are explicit messages that the leader sends to the organization about reengineering: what it means, why we are doing it, how we are going about it and what it will take. Symbols are actions that the leader performs to reinforce the content of the signals, to demonstrate that he or she lives by his or her words: assigning the company's "best and brightest" to reengineering teams, rejecting design proposals that promise only incremental improvement and removing managers who block the reengineering effort. The leader also needs to use management systems to reinforce the reengineering message.

Reengineering Needs Top Management Involvement

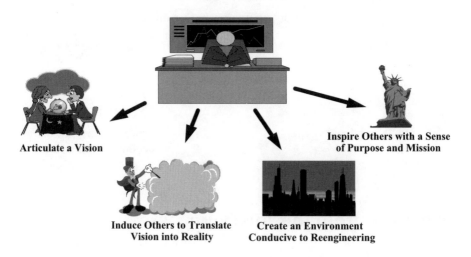

Articulate a Vision

Inspire Others with a Sense of Purpose and Mission

Induce Others to Translate Vision into Reality

Create an Environment Conducive to Reengineering

Combine Several Tasks into One Job

The most fundamental principle of reengineering is the integration and compression of fragmented activities into one process. To apply this principle in health care, organizations need to compress responsibilities for the various steps in a process and assign it to one person. This person will become the case worker and is responsible for an end-to-end process. This scenario can work for the obtainment of payment process, where one person can be responsible for certifying the patient's insurance, generating bills and following-up on unpaid accounts.

Many processes in health care cannot be integrated and assigned to one person because of the level of knowledge and skills required to perform many of the tasks. In this instance a **case team** can be organized to perform the required process. A case team is a group of people who have among them the required skills. A patient focused unit, is an example of a case team. Case team members—who previously were located in different departments—can be brought together into a single unit and given total responsibility for patient care. By integrating workers into teams, process administration overhead will reduce, the integrated *process* will have improved control because fewer people are involved and monitoring is easier. Another benefit of reengineering is that decision-making is part of the real work and not a separate function. This results in fewer delays, better customer response and greater empowerment of workers.

If a process is so complex or is dispersed in such a way that integrating them for a single person or even a small team is impossible, a single point of contact needs to be designated. This person is called a **case manager** and acts as a buffer between the still complex process and the customer. The case manager behaves with the customer as if he or she were responsible for performing the entire process, even though that is really not the case. To perform this role— that is, to be able to answer customer questions and solve customer problems— the case manager needs access to all the information systems that the people actually performing the process use, as well as the ability to contact others with questions and requests for further assistance when necessary. Case managers need to be "empowered" customer service representatives.

Perform Work When it Makes the Most Sense

Since reengineering integrates the process which is performed by a person or a team of people working closely together, work is freed from linear sequencing and the natural priority in the work can be used rather than the artificial one introduced by linearity. In reengineering, work is structured by *what needs to follow what*. "Delinearizing" processes speeds them up in two ways. One is the ability to get tasks done simultaneously, and the second is the reduction of elapsed time between early and late steps of a process. For example:

> When a patient is admitted to a facility, a demographic information sheet is entered into the computer by an admission clerk. This sheet is printed and placed in the patient's medical record. To start the utilization review process, many hospitals make a copy of the face sheet and send it to the utilization review department. The assigned staff takes the sheet and looks in the computer to determine if the patient has already been discharged. If the patient is still an inpatient, an initial utilization review is conducted. In a reengineered process, as soon as the admission clerk is has entered the patient name, reason for admission and insurance information, an e-mail message would be sent to the utilization review department. This would eliminate waiting for the physical delivery of the face sheet and having to verify the patient's status.

Perform Work When and Where it Makes the Most Sense

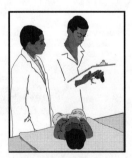

**Perform Work When it
Makes the Most Sense**

– **Steps can be performed
simultaneously**
– **Flexibility eliminates elapse time**

**Perform Work Where it
Makes the Most Sense**

– **Processes are centered around patients,
payers and accrediting agencies (instead
of around specialists)**
– **Sometimes suppliers and customers will
perform some or all of the process**

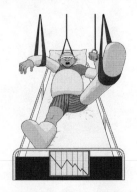

Perform Work Where it Makes the Most Sense

By shifting work across organizational boundaries, it can be performed more efficiently and with less overhead. Traditionally work has been organized around a specialist instead of around the process which specialists are trying to support. For example, hospitals are frequently organized into departments, if a patient needs to receive care from the radiology, rehabilitation and respiratory therapy departments, the patient needs to be transported to each department. By reengineering a process, services can be organized around the patient.

This principle can be applied to quality and resource management professionals by looking at where they perform most of their activities: in the quality or resource management office or on the patient units. Efficiency can be enhanced if the quality and resource management staff is decentralized among patient care areas.

Processes Have Multiple Versions

A characteristic of reengineered processes is the end of standardization. To meet the demands of customers, we need multiple versions of the same process, each one tuned to the requirement of the patients it serves. For example, the process for taking care of a patient is very similar; all patients need to be assessed and receive treatment. However, the type of assessments and treatments required for a patient experiencing an acute myocardial infarction is very different from the type of requirements of a patient having a baby. Therefore, processes with multiple versions or pathways usually begin with a "triage" step to determine which version works best in a given situation. Simple triage needs to be based on some preestablished thresholds, which will facilitate a patient being admitted to the right process.

Processes Have Multiple Versions

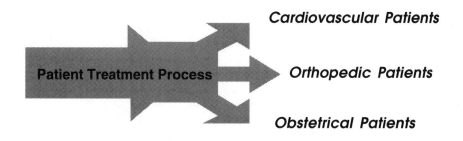

Common Changes from Reengineering

Besides being aware of reengineering principles, quality management professionals need to be aware of the changes that result from reengineering. In the book *Reengineering the Corporation* by Hammer and Champy, the following changes are presented:

- Work units change from functional department to process teams
- Jobs change from simple tasks to multi-dimensional work
- People's roles change from controlled to empowered
- Job preparation changes from training to education
- Focus on performance measures and compensation shifts from activity to results
- Advancement criteria change from performance to ability
- Values change from protective to productive
- Managers change from supervisors to coaches
- Organizational structures change from hierarchical to flat
- Executive change from scorekeepers to leaders

Role of Information Technology in Reengineering

One thing to remember about reengineering is that it cannot happen in an organization that will not change the way it thinks about information technology. Information technology is an essential enabler of reengineering, though it must be used carefully in that context. Merely installing computers in an organization does not cause it to be reengineered. In fact, misuse of automation can block reengineering if it is used to reinforce old ways of thinking and behavior patterns.

One of the big questions that needs to be asked of technology is "how can we use new technological capabilities to do things that we are not already doing?" One of the hardest parts of reengineering is recognizing the new, unfamiliar capabilities of technologies. This ability to recognize the power of modern information technology and to visualize its applications requires inductive thinking—the ability to first recognize a powerful solution and then seek the problems it might solve.

One of the important functions information technology plays in reengineering is its ability to disrupt rules about how work is conducted. For example, the belief that only specialists can perform complex work can be change by the implementation of expert systems which enable generalists to do expert work. Another important function of information technology is the ability to make data instantaneously available to a wide range of people simultaneously in many places. This accessibility to data breaks the restrictions placed on processes that have been dependent on the availability of a single file folder or medical record.

Role of Information Technology in Reengineering

Old Rule
- *Information can appear in only one place*
- *Only experts can perform complex work*
- *Businesses must choose between centralization and decentralization*
- *Managers make all decisions*
- *Field personnel need offices*
- *The best contact is personal contact*
- *You have to find out where things are*
- *Plans get revised periodically*

New Rule
- *Information can appear in two places simultaneously*
- *Generalist can do expert work*
- *Businesses can simultaneously be centralized and decentralized*
- *Decision-making is part of everyone's job*
- *Field personnel work anywhere*
- *Best contact is an effective contact*
- *Things tell you where they are*
- *Plans get revised instantaneously*

Who Will Engineer Processes?

Who should be involved in the reengineering process? How this question is answered is the key to the success of the reengineering process. Regardless of who is selected to participate in reengineering, there are distinct roles which need to be fulfilled. These roles include:

- Leader—A senior executive
- Process owner—A manager with responsibility for the specific process being reengineered.
- Reengineering team—A group of individuals dedicated to the reengineering of a particular process. The team will diagnose the existing process and oversee its redesign and implementation. A ratio of two or three process insiders to each process outsider should be maintained.
- Steering committee—A policy-making body of senior managers who develop the organization's overall reengineering strategy and monitors its progress.
- Reengineering czar—An individual responsible for developing reengineering techniques and tools within the organization and for achieving synergy across the company's separate reengineering projects.

Reengineering Quality Management

To begin, a process needs to be selected for reengineering. This is not as easy as it sounds because most people think in organizational units such as departments rather than in processes. Organizational units have names and identities while processes are invisible. For example, quality assurance, utilization review, risk management are not processes, they are departments. But what processes are performed by the quality assurance, utilization review and risk management departments? The matrix shown below possible processes performed by each department.

Utilization Review	Quality Assessment & Improvement	Continuous Quality Improvement	Risk Management	Infection Control
Case Finding	Case Finding	Case Finding	Case Finding	Case Finding
Process Review	Process Review	Process Review	Process Review	Process Review
Outcome Measurement	Outcome Measurement	Outcome Measurement	Outcome Measurement	Outcome Measurement
Variance Investigation	Variance Investigation	Variance Investigation	Variance Investigation	Variance Investigation
Data Analysis	Data Analysis	Data Analysis	Data Analysis	Data Analysis
Peer Review	Peer Review			

By identifying processes, ideas can be generated regarding how to reengineer quality management to reduce duplication of effort and increase productivity.

Case for Action

After a process is selected for reengineering, a case for action needs to be developed. This case for action communicates where we are, why we can't stay here and what we need to become. These messages are important to convey because people need a compelling reason for change. There are five main parts to a case for action:

1. Summary of the current situation and what is happening
2. The problems with continuing status quo
3. Marketplace demands
4. Explanation of why the current methods are unable to meet needs
5. Cost of inaction

The case for action should be brief, no more than five to ten pages. Here is an example of a **Case for Action** related to quality management at Hospital Anywhere:

- We are unable to meet the need of clinicians, administrators and outside agencies for accurate, timely and meaningful data. We are spending 75 percent of our time collecting data and only 10 percent of our time converting it into information. This only leaves a total of 15 percent of our time to communicate information, provide education and manage quality projects.

- With the changes in the accreditation process, the increase in capitated funding and the customers increasing demand for accountability and cost-containment, we will be unable to meet the need.

- Our current method of conducting data collection causes duplication of effort, excessive workload and frustration. This will continue since data collection is fragmented and decentralized.

- We have strong competitive and economic incentives to move as quickly as possible toward an integrated data collection process. This will result in reducing the amount of time spent on data collection to 10 percent. Allowing time to meet the demands of staff, physicians and outside agencies for information, training and quality initiatives. We will be able to convert our image from a necessary evil to a vital information support.

- If we do not make this conversion, then we will lack the flexibility to meet changing regulations and standards and information needed for managed care contract negotiation will be unavailable. This can result in non-accreditation and reduction in revenues.

Vision Statement

Once a case for action is developed a vision statement needs to be communicated. This statement describes how the organization is going to operate and outlines the kind of results expected from the reengineering effort. Additionally, it will:

- Contain the qualitative and quantitative goals
- State which process actually needs work
- Provide a yard stick for measuring progress of reengineering

This vision statement is different from the vision statements which frequently are the results of management retreats. This vision statement focuses on operations, establishes measurable objectives and may change the basis for competition in the industry.

The case for action and vision statements need to be used together because one gets people moving and the other indicates the direction. It is the leader's personal responsibility to articulate and communicate these key messages.

Reengineering Process

There is more than one way to reengineer a process. However, there are certain guidelines which have been proven useful in reengineering. These guidelines include:

- Redesigning is done best in teams
- The time between the beginning of reengineering and the initiation of the reengineered process should not exceed one year
- Start with desired results and work backwards
- Change a process, don't fix it
- Focus on processes
- Consider everything associated with the process being redesigned (job designs, organization structures, management systems, etc.)
- Expect disruption: if nothing is disrupted then no change has occurred
- Use people's values and beliefs in reengineering
- Demand dramatic results
- Eliminate all constraints on the definition of the problem and the scope of the reengineering effort
- Ignore existing corporate cultures and management attitudes
- Assign someone who understands reengineering to lead the effort
- Supply adequate resources
- Reengineering needs to be top priority
- Plan the implementation carefully

Exercise: Creating a Plan for Action

Step 1. Select one of the patient care review processes listed below
Step 2. Answer the questions listed below to formulate a plan for action

Patient Care Review Processes

- Collecting clinical information, or
- Obtaining insurance payment, or
- Analyzing and presenting clinical information

Action Plan

1. Summarize the current situation of the selected patient care review process.

2. Describe the current and anticipated problems with continuing the selected patient care review process using the current methods.

3. Describe the current and future demands being placed on this process.

4. Explain why the current methods are unable to meet these identified demands.

5. Outline the tangible and intangible costs of maintaining the status quo.

5

Moving from Chart Analysis to Data Management

In recent years, the health care industry has obtained a new appreciation of statistical thinking about quality, costs and services. By being able to statistically analyze the clinical and administrative processes which make up the health care industry many improvements can be identified and results can be quantified.

This section offers education in statistical thinking and statistical techniques for quality management professionals and administrators. Statistical thinking makes people better managers, accountants, financial analysts, health care providers, administrators and so on. It is a formal framework for systematic clarification of ambiguous and uncertain processes and provides efficiencies of thought. The end result is improved design of patient care processes and cost savings. Statistics, despite its reputation as an abstract and difficult subject, is an eminently practical one. To put analysis in proper context both study design and data collection issues are addressed. This chapter presents how to:

- Design clinical studies,
- Perform common analysis tests,
- Correlate patterns of care with patient outcomes and
- Conduct variance analysis of clinical data.

Study Design

Before any data can be collected and analyzed, a study needs to be designed. One of the major differences between chart analysis and data analysis is the fact that data analysis is trying to prove something, there is a clearly defined purpose for collecting data. To design a study, quality management professionals need to:

- State the reason for the study of a topic
- Define the problem being investigated
- Select a population to include in the study
- Choose a methodology for the study
- Calculate sample size requirements
- Determine data analysis methods
- Formulate conclusions

Each of these will be discussed in the following sections.

Reasons for Collecting Data

Before initiating a quality or resource study, the reason for collecting data needs to be understood. Otherwise, much work could be done collecting data that is of no use to the study at hand.

Knowing the Reason for a Quality/Resource Review Lets You Hit the Target

There are three main reasons for collecting data. The first is to **predict future behavior** of people or processes. For example, data about the initiation of antibiotics prior to surgery and the incidence of surgical wound infections can be used to predict a patient's chance of developing an infection if antibiotics are not administered. Studies that are designed to predict future behaviors frequently use **inferential statistics** to make predictions based on the probability of a certain behavior or outcome occurring.

The second reason for collecting data is to **detect changes** in a process. For example, at a local hospital the average length of stay for patients with community-acquired bacterial pneumonia is 5.2 days. However, during the month of December, the average length of stay reduced to 4.5 days. This shift downward relative to the previously observed behavior would trigger investigation into the reasons for the reduction.

The final reason for data collection is to **share or communicate information**. For example, if a sequence plot graph showing the number of medication errors that occur every day is posted in the pharmacy and updated every day, the pharmacists can see the effects of the medication distribution process. This visual reporting of the medication distribution process data makes communication very easy.

Problem Definition

Problem definition is simply a statement of the purpose for the quality management study. This problem is usually stated as a goal. For example, the reason to study the care of patients with congestive heart failure is to reduce the length of stay, or reduce the incidence of pulmonary edema, or reduce the number of readmissions during a specific timeframe. Without this purpose, data is just being collected to be collected. A clearly defined purpose provides the context for data analysis. Once a problem has been identified, hypotheses about how the problem may be solved need to be developed. *A hypothesis states a belief or educated guess about the relationship between specific data elements*. Forming hypotheses is important because it provides the logic for consensus building, directs information requirements and guides the selection of analytical tools.

Once the problem definition is complete and hypotheses are stated, quality management professionals are ready to define the study's population.

Population Definition

Population definition is an important part of study design because it facilitates consistent decisions by data collectors regarding whom to include in a study, identifies the sample sizes needed and describes to whom the conclusions can be applied. The objective of the population definition is to create a homogeneous sample, enhancing the accuracy and validity of analysis. An example of a population description for a fractured hip critical pathway initiative might be:

> All patients over the age of 65 years admitted through the emergency department with a primary diagnosis of closed intertrochanteric or subtrochanteric fracture (ICD-9-CM: 820.21, 820.22) due to trauma. All patients will receive surgical intervention for fractures. Patients with active infectious processes or malignancies will be excluded from the study.

Study Methodology

The study methodology consists of at least two parts, one is the type of study being conducted and the data elements being selected for inclusion in a study.

Types of Studies

The simplest way of collecting data is to record outcomes generated by the process as it evolves. These outcomes can be measured systematically at predetermined instants. This entire process is called simple observation. Many occurrence screening and utilization review programs use a simple observation method of evaluating the effectiveness and efficiency of a clinical process.

In reality, collecting data can be time consuming and expensive. To facilitate maximum information at minimum cost most health care organizations us a sample survey method of data collection. **The sample survey consists of selecting a sample of elements for measurement from a universe of elements. A universe refers to the collection of all elements of interest, such as patients who have congestive heart failure during a specified time period. A sample is a collection of elements drawn from the universe.** Samples are studied by collecting data, such as answers to questions, observation of certain behaviors and so forth. For example, to determine if a medical record meets the pertinence of medical records requirements, a questionnaire is developed asking specific questions about the timing of completion and the content of a patient's chart.

The final type of study is experimentation, which is the study of the effects of change in a limited environment that is, to some degree, under the control of the experimenter. Although experiments help explain the effects of changes, their results can not always be immediately generalized to practical situations because of the control exercised in the experiment may not be possible in the real world. However, field experiments in real-world settings, such as a drug trial with experimental medications produce results more readily applicable to immediate problems. Using the experimental approach to determine causation in the real world is called **quasi-experimentation**.

For a study to be considered experimental there needs to be at least a treatment, an outcome measure, units of assignment and some comparison from which change can be inferred and hopefully attributed to the treatment. There are three types of quasi-experiments, nonequivalent group designs, interrupted time-series designs and correlational-designs.

Nonequivalent group design is typically one in which responses of a treatment group and a comparison group are measured before and after a treatment. This would be the case where two groups of patients are compared to each other and outcome data is collected at the beginning and end of the inpatient service. For example, patients with congestive heart failure can be divided into groups which receive ACE inhibitors and those which do not receive this medication. By comparing the severity levels of each group at the time of admission and then at discharge, quality improvement professionals are using nonequivalent group design to determine if ACE inhibitors is a causal force of severity level.

Interrupted time-series design is used when quality professionals compare measures of performance taken at many time intervals before a treatment with measures taken at many intervals afterwards. For example, the length of stay for patient with congestive heart failure is measured for three months prior to pathway implementation and then for three months after implementation. The comparison between the lengths of stay will help determine if causal inferences can be made for the developed pathway.

Finally, **correlational-designs**, also called passive observational methods, most often refers to efforts at causal inference based on measures taken all at one time, with differential levels of both effects and exposures to presumed causes, being measured as they occur naturally, without any experimental interventions. For example, the methods described in the pathway development section of this book show the correlational design.

Although, any of the three types of studies can be used by quality management professionals to measure quality and to monitor clinical processes a decision needs to be made regarding what type of study will meet the needs of the organization within the available resources and time constraints.

Types of Data

One thing to remember is that we seldom have complete knowledge of a process, nor can we expect to exercise complete control over every step in a process . Fortunately, most processes can be managed by exercising control at just a few critical steps. A key ingredient in managing and improving health care processes is to stay in touch with the critical steps by collecting relevant measurements. Such measurements are called data.

Data should be collected systematically over a long period of time from the truly critical steps of a process. Studies of the evolution of a process over time are called longitudinal studies. More precisely, a longitudinal study consists of:

- Collection of data from a process over time
- Comparison of data from different time periods
- Documentation of variation over time
- Evaluation of changes in behavior of the process

The critical pathway process described earlier in this book is an example of a longitudinal study. By thinking longitudinally, we can focus on those aspects of the process critical for decision making. By limiting attention to the points that make the most difference, people will work at peak efficiency, avoiding wasted effort.

Process Data

Process data is one of the basic types of data found in the health care industry. This data relates to the sequence of steps taken by caregivers to cure or improve the health of a patient. To measure the quality of a process, data must be collected. Data are measures of characteristics of a process. For example, to monitor the process of diagnosing pneumonia, the number and timing of chest x-rays are recorded for each patient with a diagnosis of pneumonia. By aggregating the data, clinicians can understand at least one process variable in the diagnosing of pneumonia.

Since a process is a sequence of steps taken to achieve a goal. The scientific study of a process seeks to model each step and the relationships among the steps. A successful model yields understanding of the fundamental causes of the variations in the process. Activities leading to such an understanding are called **process analysis**.

Ideally, a model also yields accurate predictions of the future behavior of the process. If so, the model can be used as a basis for **process control**. Control may mean keeping the process outcomes near a predetermined "target" so the output from the process is dependable. This kind of control, which is also called **process regulation**, is typical in laboratory calibration and process improvement efforts.

To understand process control and improvement, a clinician must be aware of "Shewhart's cycle," which outlines the continuous process improvement cycle. This cycle consists of planning, doing, checking and acting. This cycle is the basis of many of the continuous improvement initiatives found in the health care industry.

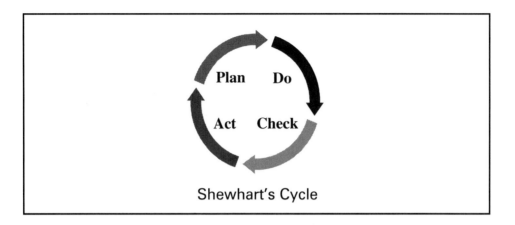

Shewhart's Cycle

Continuous Data

To be analyzed statistically, data must be numerical or coded numerically. Even things that are not strictly "measurable" must be reduced to cold figures. For example, patient satisfaction is captured using an numeric rating system instead of a series of statements. Numeric measurements give us a concrete handle on problems that no amount of speculation can replace.

Categorical Data

Another important type of data is categorical data, data that is arranged in classes or categories. These categories are determined by classifying elements into groups according to a common attribution. For example, all people who have congestive heart failure and receive ACE inhibitors are in the same category. By counting the number of elements or cases in this category we are dealing with categorical data.

When a collection of data values becomes available for analysis, it is important to understand the basic characteristics of the collection. This understanding helps determine the best type of analysis to use on the available data.

Sampling

An important study design issue in causal research is the selection and size of a sample. This issue is important because it impacts the level of confidence in the inferences made from available data and promotes study validity.

Sample size is influenced by the population's degree of homogeneity, the desired level of confidence and/or the type of statistical test being used.

The homogeneity of the population is the degree of sameness within a population. For example, if 90 percent of patients with pneumonia receive a chest x-ray in the emergency department, there is a high degree of homogeneity. However, if 20 different antibiotic regimens are used to treat patients with pneumonia then there is a low degree of homogeneity.

The level of confidence is the probability that an incorrect assumption is accepted. For example, clinicians may want to be 95 percent sure that giving an antibiotic two hours prior to an incision will reduce the probability of the patient developing a surgical wound infection.

The type of statistical test influences the sample size because certain tests have minimum population sizes established. For example, to perform a z-test, which determines if there is a difference between two different populations, a minimum sample size for each population is 30.

Samples must be selected randomly, regardless of their size. Every case must have an equal chance of being included in the sample in order to provide an accurate reflection of the total population and serve as an adequate foundation for statistical tests. Clinicians can use various methods for choosing cases, including simple random, systematic random, stratified random and cluster sampling.

1. *Simple Random Sample:* A portion of items (cases) selected from a population in a manner which ensures all items have an equal chance or probability of being chosen.

2. *Systematic Random Sample:* A sampling method where every *n*th number of items is selected for the sample. *"N"* is a predetermined constant number of cases. For example, every seventh case will be included in the sample.

3. *Stratified Random Sample:* Selecting a portion of a population by sub-dividing it according to specified characteristics, then randomly choosing cases from each sub-group.

4. *Cluster Random Sample:* A two stage sampling process which first sub-divides the population into groups or clusters according to a specific characteristic, then a random sample of clusters is chosen. A portion of subjects within each cluster are selected. This sampling method is most often used in epidemiological research and commonly based on geographic areas or districts.

Data Analysis

Once data has been collected, quality management professionals need to be able to tell a story using the collected data. This story needs to describe the current situation, show how the elements or factors relate to one another and predict what will probably happen in the future. The storytelling method is called data analysis.

The rest of this chapter will be spent explaining how to analyze available data. To facilitate this process, the data shown below will be used.

Case Study

At a medical center located in the heartland of America, a study was developed to test the impact of calcium channel blockers on patients with systolic dysfunction congestive heart failure. The study results would be shared with the pharmacy and therapeutic committee, internal medicine department and emergency department. The table below shows the raw data collected during the retrospective review.

Congestive Heart Failure: Use of Calcium Channel Blockers											
Patient	Day 1	Day 2	Day 3	Day 4	Day 5	Day 6	Day 7	ACE Used	LOS	Readmit w/i 30 days	Pulm. Ed.
1								No	2		
2		X	X	X	X	X	X	Yes	13		Yes
3								Yes	3		
4								Yes	3		
5		X	X	X	X	X	X	Yes	8		
6								No	6		
7								No	6		
8								Yes	10		
9								No	2	CHF	
10								Yes	2		
11				X	X	X	X	No	11	CHF	
12								Yes	12		Yes
13								Yes	2	CHF	
14	X		X	X	X	X	X	Yes	6		
15			X	X				Yes	12		

Measurements of Central Tendencies

To begin data analysis it is important to understand how data is distributed within a selected population or sample size. This distribution will allow clinicians to describe the population in numerical (nominal) terms. Numeric or frequency methods of analysis are often called descriptive statistics. Descriptive statistics identifies the common attributes of a given set of data and focuses on central tendencies, variations and frequency measurements. These measurements are important because they allow for summarization of information and provide essential data required for more sophisticated tests.

Frequency Distribution

When summarizing raw data, it is useful to distribute the data into groups or categories and determine the number of individuals belonging to each group. By counting the number of cases in each category (categorical data) we are determining the **frequency distribution**. Frequency distributions show a clear "overall" picture from which vital relationships between data elements can become evident. Frequency distributions should be used to demonstrate "patterns of care."

Examples of patterns of care for electrolytes are "pre-admission only," "day of surgery" and "pre-admission and first post-operative day." Once patterns of care are identified, analysts need to count the number of cases (or frequency) which demonstrate each pattern of care. The result of these counts is the frequency distribution. **It is important to remember that the sum of each category does not exceed the total number of cases in the sample.**

To formulate a frequency distribution, clinicians or analysts should:

Step 1.   Select categories for stratifying data

Step 2.   Sum the number of values in each group

EXERCISE: Using the data in the case study calculate the frequency distribution for patients not on calcium channel blockers.

Step 1.   The stratification of this group is (1) patients on calcium channel blockers and ACE inhibitors (2) patients on calcium channel blockers without ACE inhibitors and (3) patients not on calcium channel blockers.

Step 2.   Calculate the number of values in each group

Category of Groups	Frequency Distribution
Patients on calcium channel blockers and ACE inhibitors	
Patients on calcium channel blockers without ACE inhibitors	
Patients not on calcium channel blockers or ACE inhibitors	
Patient not on calcium channel blockers but on ACE inhibitors	

Histograms

Histograms are graphic tools for displaying distributions of large sets of data. Histograms group the data into a relatively small number of classes and show the frequencies of the classes. In the statistical literature, several somewhat different displays are called histograms. We distinguish among three types: frequency histograms, relative frequency histograms and density histograms.

Frequency histograms, the most basic histograms, are graphic displays of frequency distributions. All they require is grouping the data into classes, counting the number of observations in each class and making a plot.

EXERCISE: Using the data in the frequency distribution table above, plot a frequency histogram.

Category of Groups	Frequency Distribution
Patients on calcium channel blockers and ACE inhibitors	
Patients on calcium channel blockers without ACE inhibitors	
Patients not on calcium channel blockers or ACE inhibitors	
Patient not on calcium channel blockers but on ACE inhibitors	

Dotplots

A way to display this data is called a dotplot, which consists of a horizontal scale on which dots are placed to show the numerical values of the data points. If a data value repeats, the dots are piled up at the location, one dot for each repetition. Statisticians say that a dotplot displays the distribution of the data. The dotplot is especially useful when the distribution behavior of a relatively small set of numbers needs to be displayed. It shows the position of the data points on a number line and displays frequencies.

EXERCISE: Using the data in the same data in the case study, plot the length of stay for each data element in each category.

Step 1. List the length of stay for each case which meets the category criteria in the first column.

Category of Groups	Lengths of Stay Values
Patients on calcium channel blockers and ACE inhibitors	
Patients on calcium channel blockers without ACE inhibitors	
Patients not on calcium channel blockers or ACE inhibitors	
Patients not on calcium channel blockers but on ACE inhibitors	

Step 2. Place channel blockers in the bottom row.

Step 3 On the left hand column, write the possible lengths of stay from 0-14. This will represent the different lengths of stay.

Step 4. Plot a dot for each data element on the intersection of each category and length of stay.

14			
12			
10			
8			
6			
4			
2			
0			
On calcium channel and ACE	On calcium channel without ACE	Not on calcium channel or ACE	Not on calcium channel but on ACE

Mean

The mean is the arithmetic average of all values in a group or population. It is symbolized as a "μ in entire populations or a "$\overline{x}$" in sample populations. The way to compute the mean for a group is:

Step 1   Add all the values in the group.

Step 2. Divide by the number of values in the group.

EXERCISE: Use data found in the case study and compute the mean (average) length of stay.

Step 1.

Step 2.

Geometric Mean

The geometric mean is frequently used in medicine and epidemiology to describe the mean of diagnostic related groups. It is a logarithmic mean and is symbolized by a "GM" or "G." Geometric means are considered less sensitive to extreme variation in the group than arithmetic means. To compute the geometric mean you will:

Step 1. Multiply together all the values in the group.

Step 2. Compute the root of the product using the number of values in the set as the root.

EXERCISE: Use data found in the case study and compute the mean (average) length of stay.

Step 1.

Step 2. $\sqrt{}$

Let's combine frequency distribution with arithmetic mean. This will present a different dimension to the same data.

EXERCISE: Use the data found in the case study and compute the mean length of stay for each group.

Step 1. Use the four groups designated in the previous exercise

Step 2. Add together all the lengths of stay for each group

Step 3. Divide by the number of values in each group

Step 4. Use a dot plot to demonstrate the distribution of lengths of stay

Step 5. Mark on the graph the average length of stay for each category

14			
12			
10			
8			
6			
4			
2			
0			
On calcium channel and ACE	On calcium channel without ACE	Not on calcium channel or ACE	Not on calcium channel but on ACE

Median

The median is the middle value in a group which contains an odd number of values. If the group contains an even number of values, the median is defined as the average of the two middle values. The median is used frequently in run charts as a benchmark value. Although there is no conventional symbol for it, an "M" or "Md" is sometimes used. To compute the median for a group you will:

Step 1. Order all the values from least to most (or vice versa).

Step 2. Find the middle value. Half of the values will be larger and half will be smaller than this amount.

Step 3. If there are an even number of values in the group, compute the mean of the middle two values.

EXERCISE: Using the data found in the case study determine the median for the length of stay.

Step 1.

Step 2.

Step 3.

Mode

The mode is the most frequently occurring ("most popular") value in a given group. Clinicians can use this value while developing critical pathways to demonstrate the most popular forms of treatments or the most common patient outcomes. To compute the mode of a population, you will:

Step 1. Count the number of incidents of each value in the group.

Step 2. Select the most frequently occurring value. If there is a tie for the most frequent value, they are both considered the mode.

EXERCISE: Using the data in the case study, determine the mode of the length of stay.

Step 1. Determine the length of stay groups. Enter these values in the Length of Stay column.

Step 2. Count the number of values in each group.

Step 3. Select the mode.

STATISTICAL TEST	FORMULA	RECOMMENDED DATA PRESENTATION
Mean	$\dfrac{(x_1) + (x_2) + (x...)}{n}$	Table, histogram, bar graph
Geometric Mean	$\sqrt[n]{(x_1)(x_2).....(x_n)}$	Table, histogram, bar graph

STATISTICAL TEST	FORMULA	RECOMMENDED DATA PRESENTATION
Median	The middle number in a set after they are placed in ascending or descending order.	Table, central tendency in run chart, histogram, bar graph
Mode	The most frequently occurring value in a set of numbers	Table, histogram, bar graph

Central tendency test summary.

Descriptive Analysis

Hypothesis: The timing of physical therapy impacts the length of stay.

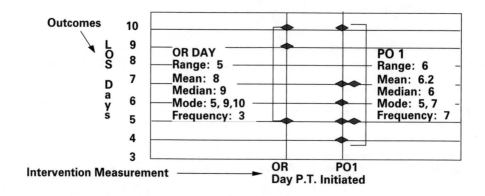

Measures of Variation

Even though central tendency computations start to describe the target population, they do not give the whole picture. Range and standard deviation are common measures of variations and describe the amount of diversity within a given population.

Range

The most elementary measure of variation is the range. The range is the difference between the largest and smallest values in a group. The purpose of the range is to illustrate wide variances in values. Clinicians can use range to determine if there are variations in practice or patient outcomes. The larger the range, the greater the variation among members of the group. To compute the range for a population, simply:

Step 1.   Rank all values from smallest to largest.
Step 2.   Subtract the smallest value from the largest value.

EXERCISE: Using the data in the case study, determine the range of the lengths of stay.

Step 1.
Step 2.

Standard Deviation

Stand ard deviation is the most common measurement of variation used for analyzing healthcare data. It is defined as the positive square root of the variance and measures the spread of data about the mean. To make the standard deviation meaningful, clinicians need to know the mean for the group.

To compute the standard deviation, you will:

Step 1.   Compute the mean for the group.
Step 2.   Subtract the mean from each value to form the deviation.
Step 3.   Square each deviation.
Step 4.   Add the squared deviations together.
Step 5.   Subtract 1 from the number of values in the group.
Step 6.   Divide the sum of the squared deviation in step 4 by the difference obtained in step 5 (***This is the variance***).
Step 7.   Take the square root of the variance in step 6.

STATISTICAL TEST	FORMULA	RECOMMENDED DATA DISPLAY
Range	Largest value - Smallest value	Footnote, table, x-axis for histograms and bar graphs
Standard Deviation	$\sigma = \sqrt{\dfrac{\Sigma(X - \bar{X})^2}{n - 1}}$	Table, line graph, control charts limits

Statistical tests for measuring variation.

EXERCISE: Using the case study information, determine the standard deviation for the length of stay.

Step 1   2+13+3+3+8+6+6+10+2+2+11+12+2+6+12= 98/15 = 6.5

Step 2.   Subtract the mean from each value to form the deviation.

Step 3.   Square each deviation.

Step 4.   Add the squared deviations together.

Patient	Length of Stay	Avg. Length of Stay	Deviation	Squared Deviation
1	2	-	=	
2	13	-	=	+
3	3	-	=	+
4	3	-	=	+
5	8	-	=	+
6	6	-	=	+
7	6	-	=	+
8	10	-	=	+
9	2	-	=	+
10	2	-	=	+
11	11	-	=	+
12	12	-	=	+
13	2	-	=	+
14	6	-	=	+
15	12	-	=	+
TOTAL				=

Step 5.   15-1=14

Step 6.   Divide the sum of the squared deviation in step 4 by the difference obtained in step 5 (***This is the variance***).

Step 7.   Take the square root of the variance in step 6.

$$\sqrt{}$$

Run Charts

One visual way quality management coordinators can display variance data is to construct a run chart. This chart is used to identify special causes of process variation in the form of trends, shifts or other non-random patterns. The steps in drawing a run chart are:

Step 1. Draw a vertical and horizontal axis on a piece of graph paper.

Step 2. Label the vertical axis with the name of the number being plotted.

Step 3. Label the horizontal axis with the unit of time or order in which the numbers were collected (for example, 1, 2, 3, etc.).

Step 4. Determine the scale of the vertical axis. Pick a number 20 percent larger than the largest value and 20 percent smaller than the smallest value. Label the axis in equal intervals between these two numbers.

Step 5. Plot the numbers on the graph number by number, preserving the order in which they occurred.

Step 6. Connect the points on the graph.

Step 7. Find the median of the plotted numbers.

Step 8. Draw the median on the graph.

Step 9. Apply special cause rules to data.

Rule 1: Eight or more consecutive points either above or below the median is an indicator of a possible shift in the level of the process. Ignore values on the median.

Rule 2: Lines between successive points alternately going up and down 13 times indicate possible non-randomness. If the value of two or more successive points is the same, the rule does not apply.

Rule 3: Six lines between successive points all going up or all going down are indicators of possible trends. If the value of two or more successive points is the same, ignore the lines connecting those values when counting: like values do not make or break a trend.

Rule 4: Apply the astronomic value test. The task is to detect a blatantly obvious different value.

Control Charts

Control charts show what a process is capable of and when a potential improvement in a process has been successful. To be able to construct a control chart, quality management professionals will need to know the mean and the standard deviations for a group. The mean value will become the center line. By adding the standard deviation to the mean value, an upper control limit of 1 SD is established. By subtracting the standard deviation from the mean value, a lower control limit of 1 SD is established.

By plotting each deviation from the mean on the chart, you can determine the degree a process is in control.

Descriptive Analysis: Run Chart

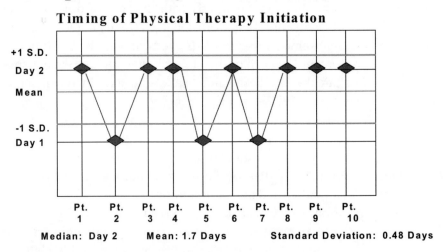

Measures of Nominal Data

Nominal data does not measure the actual counts or frequency of occurrences. Rather, it measures proportions, ratios and rates. These methods allow clinicians to describe clusters of data relative to the whole group. Proportions and rates can assist clinicians in describing the prevalence of an intervention or patient outcome.

Proportion and Percentage

A proportion is the number of cases with a specified characteristic or group of characteristics divided by the total number of cases in the group. Proportions are useful in determining the frequency of a particular occurrence.

Proportions are especially useful for analyzing patient incident reports, adverse drug reactions and patient complaints. A proportion can be converted into a percentage by simply multiplying it by 100. To determine a proportion, you would:

Step 1.   Divide the number of observations with a specific characteristic by the total number of observations (both with and without that characteristic).

Rate

A rate is similar to a proportion except it is multiplied by a base number and is computed for a specified period of time. The base number is usually 100, 1000, 10,000 or 100,000 and is selected so that the smallest proportion has at least one digit to the left of the decimal point. It is important to use the same base number when comparing one rate to another. Rates are generally used to present nosocomial infections. To determine a rate, clinicians will:

Step 1.   Divide the number of observations with a specific characteristic by the total number of observations within the specified time period.

Step 2.   Multiply the proportion by a constant base number.

STATISTICAL TEST	FORMULA	RECOMMENDED DATA DISPLAY
Proportion	$Proportion = \dfrac{a}{a+b}$	Pie chart, line graph
Percentage	$Percentage = \dfrac{a}{a+b} \times 100\%$	Pie chart, line graph, bar chart
Rate	$Rate = \dfrac{a}{a+b} \times k$	Line graph, bar chart, histogram

Summary of statistical tests for nominal data.

Inferential Statistics

The previously presented statistical tests tell clinicians what the population looks like but not why or how they arrived at this point. The next group of statistical tests allows clinicians to test their established hypotheses by making comparisons among different populations and correlating the interventions with outcomes. These inferential statistics tests can be applied to the collected data to determine why and how an outcome occurred.

Certain concepts are pivotal in understanding inferential statistics. They are:

1. Probability

2. Rule of addition

3. Rule of multiplication

4. Significance level

5. Z-score

6. Errors of hypothesis testing

7. Confidence interval

By understanding these key concepts, clinicians will be better equipped to perform and interpret inferential statistical tests such as chi square, t-test, Fisher exact, z-test, ANOVA and correlation coefficient.

Probability

Probability measures the likelihood that a specific event or outcome will occur. It is expressed as a ratio, which is computed by dividing the number of times a result occurs by the total number of cases. If the outcome is sure to occur, the probability is one (1), if the outcome cannot occur it is zero (0). Understanding probability is important because it is a basic principle used in chi square and Fisher exact tests to show if a specific critical pathway outcome occurs by chance or as a result of a pathway.

To compute probability, clinicians will:

Step 1.   Count the number of times an event occurs.

Step 2.   Divide the number of times an event occurs by the total number of values in the group.

EXERCISE: Using the data in the case study, determine the probability of a patient having a length of stay of six days.

Rule of Addition

The Rule of Addition is used to describe the probability of at least one mutually exclusive event occurring when two or more types of independent events are possible. To compute probability using the Rule of Addition, clinicians will:

      Step 1.   Compute the probability for each mutually exclusive group.

      Step 2.   Add all probabilities together.

EXERCISE: Using the case study data, determine the probability for a patient developing either pulmonary edema or being readmitted within 30 days post-discharge.

      Step 1.

      Step 2.

Rule of Multiplication

The Rule of Multiplication is used to determine the probability of two or more independent events all occurring. This is computed by multiplying all of the individual probabilities together. To perform this computation:

      Step 1.   Compute the probability for each independent event

      Step 2.   Multiply together all probabilities from step 1.

EXAMPLE: Determine the probability of a patient having both pulmonary edema and being readmitted within 30 days post discharge.

      Step 1.

      Step 2.

Level of Significance

Level of significance is the probability of observing a test result equal to or more extreme than the event can actually be observed from chance alone. This probability is represented by the letter P (for probability) and is a number between zero (0) and one (1). The smaller the significance level the more stringent the test. The significance level is established in advance of the test and is sometimes referred to as a critical test value or alpha level. Commonly used significance levels are 0.05 (1 chance in 20), 0.01 (1 chance in 100), or 0.001 (1 chance in 1,000).

It is important to understand significance level because statistical tests such as t-tests, z-tests, chi square and Fisher exact tests use the significance to decide whether to accept or reject the null hypothesis.

Z-Score

The z-score expresses the deviation from the mean in standard deviation units and is synonymous with terms such as z transformation, a standard score or a critical ratio. Z-score is based on the *central limit theorem*, a rule stating that the sampling distribution of means from any population will be normal for large samples. Converting actual values to z-score allows clinicians to use the area of the normal distribution curve to determine the probability of occurrence for a given value. To compute the z-score, clinicians will:

Step 1. Compute the mean for the group.
Step 2. Compute standard deviation.
Step 3. Subtract the mean from the designated value.
Step 4. Divide the answer from step 3 by the standard deviation.

EXAMPLE: Using the case study data, determine the z-score for the length of stay of six days

Step 1.
Step 2.
Step 3.
Step 4.

Errors of Hypothesis Testing

In hypothesis terminology, the most common hypothesis is called a null hypothesis. This hypothesis states there is no difference between the hypothesized value and the population mean. (Null means "no difference") The other type of hypothesis is called an alternative hypothesis and is a statement disagreeing with the null hypothesis. If the null hypothesis is rejected as a result of statistical analysis, then the alternative hypothesis is the conclusion. If there is not sufficient evidence to reject the null hypothesis, it is not accepted but is retained as a hypothesis. The null hypothesis is symbolized by H_0 while the alternative hypothesis is symbolized by H_1.

There are two types of errors made in a test of hypotheses. One error type results from rejecting a null hypothesis when it is true and is called a type I error The probability of making a type I error is called the alpha value (α).

The second type of hypothesis error is a type II error, and results from failing to reject the null hypothesis when it is false or not rejecting the null hypothesis when the alternative hypothesis is true. The probability of a type II error is symbolized by the Greek letter beta (β).

Another important concept related to hypothesis testing is power. Beth Dawson-Saunders and Robert Trapp write, "Power is defined as the probability of rejecting the null hypothesis when it is false or of concluding the alternative hypothesis when it is true." The power of the test is expressed as $1 - \beta$.

Confidence Intervals

Confidence Interval (CI) is the range of values having a given probability of containing an unknown sample parameter (mean or proportion)

given a specific significance level. Common confidence intervals are 90 percent, 95 percent, and 99 percent. The boundaries of the confidence interval are called confidence limits and are the values having a given probability that the unknown parameter is located between them. To express confidence intervals and confidence limits a clinician might state, "there is a 95 percent chance that the average length of stay for patients with congestive heart failure will be between four to ten days."

STATISTICAL TEST	FORMULA	RECOMMENDED DATA DISPLAY
Probability	$P = \dfrac{\text{\# of events}}{\text{\# of possible}}$	Table, footnote
Rule of Addition	P(A or B) = P(A) + P(B)	Table, footnote
Rule of Multiplication	P(A and B) = P(A) x P(B)	Table, footnote
Z- score	$z = \dfrac{X - \mu}{\sigma}$	Not applicable
Level of Significance	The probability of an event occurring equal to or more frequently than the event can occur from chance alone.	Footnote
Type I error	Rejecting a null hypothesis when it is true	Not applicable
Type II error	Failing to reject the null hypothesis when it is false or not rejecting the null hypothesis when the alternative hypothesis is true.	Not applicable

Summary of foundational concepts for inferential statistics

Chi-Square

The most commonly used statistical test for comparing frequency or proportions of two or more independent groups is chi square. Chi square is used to test the null hypothesis by determining the probability of a difference occurring between the groups. It is also used to test the dependent relationship between the process variables within each group. To perform a chi square test, each group involved must be mutually exclusive and the expected frequency for each group must be equal to or greater than five.

To perform a chi square test, clinicians should use a chi square critical value chart. An abbreviated critical value chart is shown on the next page.

Degree of Freedom	Level of Significance			
	0.10	0.05	0.01	0.001
1	2.706	3.841	6.635	10.828
2	4.605	5.991	9.210	13.816
3	6.251	7.815	11.345	16.266
4	7.779	9.488	13.277	18.467
5	9.236	11.071	15.086	20.515

Critical value chart.

To perform a chi square test, clinicians follow these procedures:

Step 1. Formulate a null and alternative hypothesis about the relationship between a treatment modality and the patient outcome.

Step 2. Select the desired level of significance

Step 3. Compute the degree of freedom for the test.
$$df = (\# \text{ of rows} - 1) \times (\# \text{ of columns} - 1)$$

Step 4. Label each column with dependent outcomes and column for total.

Step 5. Label each row with processes variables and a row for total.

Step 6. Place frequencies in the table for each event.

Step 7. Add all frequencies found in the rows and place in the total column.

Step 8. Add all frequencies found in the columns and place in the total row.

Step 9. Compute the expected probability for each cell by multiplying the row total by the column total and dividing by the grand total.

Step 10. Subtract the expected frequency from the actual frequency.

Step 11. Square the difference between the observed and the expected frequencies of each cell.

Step 12. Divide the squared value of each cell in step 11 by the expected value for the cell.

Step 13. Add all the quotients together.

Step 14. The critical value is the number located where the degree of freedom row intersects with the level of significance column. If the sum is greater than the critical value the null hypothesis is rejected.

EXAMPLE: Determine if there is a relationship between calcium channel blockers and pulmonary edema.

Step 1. *Null Hypothesis*: Patients with congestive heart failure who are given calcium channel blockers do *not* have a greater risk of developing pulmonary edema.

Alternative Hypothesis: Patients with congestive heart failure who are given calcium channel blockers do have a greater risk of developing pulmonary edema.

Step 2. Significance level for chi square will be 0.05.

Step 3. Degree of freedom : (2 -1) X (2 -1) = 1

Step 4. See column headings.

Steps 4-8	Cases with Pulmonary Edema	Cases without Pulmonary Edema	Total # of cases
Cases with Calcium Channel Blockers			
Cases without Calcium Channel Blockers			
Total # of cases			

Step 5. See row headings.

Step 6. Place frequency of each category of cases in corresponding table cells.

Step 7. Add rows.

Step 8. Add columns.

Step 9. Compute expected frequencies for each cell.

Step 9	Cases with Pulmonary Edema	Cases without Pulmonary Edema	Total # of cases
Cases with Calcium Channel Blockers			
Cases without Calcium Channel Blockers			
Total # of cases			

Step 10. Subtract the expected frequency from the actual.

Step 10	Cases with Pulmonary Edema	Cases without Pulmonary Edema	Total # of cases
Cases with Calcium Channel Blockers			
Cases without Calcium Channel Blockers			
Total # of cases			

Step 11. + + + =
Step 12. 3.841
Step 13. The null hypothesis is

Fisher Exact Test

The ***Fisher exact test*** is a probability test for a two by two contingency table, when the sample size is too small to use the chi-square test. If any expected frequency is less than two or if more than 20 percent of the expected frequencies are less than five, then the Fisher exact test should be used.

Clinicians should understand the concept of factorials prior to performing the Fisher exact test. Factorials are the product of all positive integers from 1 to a given number and are usually written n!. The factorial values for zero (0) and one (1) are special cases (both equal 1).

Example: 4! (read four factorial) is (4)(3)(2)(1) = 24.

The steps to follow in performing a Fisher exact test are:

Step 1.   Formulate null and alternative hypotheses.

Step 2.   Select the desired level of significance.

Step 3.   Label each column with dependent outcomes and column for total.

Step 4.   Label each row with process variables and a row for total.

Step 5.   Place frequencies in the table for each event.

Step 6.   Add all frequencies found in the rows and place in the total column.

Step 7.   Add all frequencies found in the columns and place in the total row.

Step 8.   Compute individually the factorials for the sums of row 1, row 2, column 1 and column 2, then multiply all factorial values together

$$(a + b) ! (c + d) ! (a + c) ! (b + d) !$$

Step 9.   Compute individual factorials for each cell as well as for the sum of all cell values. Multiply all resulting factorial values together.

$$a ! b ! c ! d ! n !$$

Step 10. Divide the product of step 8 by the product of step 9.

Step 11. Convert the contingency table to show more extreme observed frequencies. The smallest frequency must be reduced to one (1), however the totals for all the rows and columns must stay the same.

Step 12. Repeat steps 8 through 10 using the new contingency table.

Step 13. Convert the contingency table to show more extreme observed frequencies. The smallest frequency must be reduced to zero (0), however the totals for all rows and columns must stay the same.

Step 14. Repeat steps 8 through 10 using the new contingency table.

Step 15. Add the quotients from steps 10, 12, and 14 together.

Step 16. Compare the sum of step 15 with the appropriate critical value. The critical value is the number located where the degree of freedom row intersects with the level of significance column. If the sum of step 15 is greater than the critical value then the null hypothesis is rejected.

	Outcome A	Outcome B	Row Totals
Independent Variable A	A	B	A + B
Independent Variable B	C	D	C + D
Column Total	A + C	B + D	A + B + C + D = n

Fisher exact test template.

EXAMPLE: Determine if there is a relationship between the calcium channel blockers and pulmonary edema.

Step 1.   Null Hypothesis: Patients with congestive heart failure who receive calcium channel blockers are not at any greater risk of having pulmonary edema. Alternative Hypothesis: Patients with congestive heart failure who receive calcium channel blocker are at greater risk of having pulmonary edema.

Step 2.   Significance level for Fisher exact test will be 0.05.

Step 3.   See headings for columns.

Step 4.   See headings for rows.

Steps 4-8	Cases with Pulmonary Edema	Cases without Pulmonary Edema	Total # of cases
Cases with Calcium Channel Blockers			
Cases without Calcium Channel Blockers			
Total # of cases			

Step 5.   Place values in table.

Step 6.   Add rows and place total in right column.

   + =

   + =

Step 7.   Add columns   + =

             + =

+ =

Step 8.   ! ! ! =

Step 9.   ! ! ! ! =

Step 10.   /   =

Step 11. Convert contingency table to an extreme condition of 1.

Step 12. (! ! !) / (! ! ! !) =

Step 12	Cases with Pulmonary Edema	Cases without Pulmonary Edema	Total # of cases
Cases with Calcium Channel Blockers			
Cases without Calcium Channel Blockers			
Total # of cases			

Step 13. Convert contingency table to an extreme condition of 0.

Step 14. (! ! !) /(! ! ! !) =

Step 15. +   +   =

Step 16.   0.05

Step 17. The null hypothesis is

T-Test

T-tests are used to compare the mean of one group against a norm or to compare two groups' means to determine the probability of a significance difference existing between the groups. Another use of the t-test is to determine whether a correlation coefficient or a regression coefficient is zero (0). One type of t-test is presented below as an example.

To perform this test, the sample must have normal distribution. Two strengths of the t-test are the ability to test:

1. Small sample sizes (less than 30 cases).
2. When the standard deviation is unknown.

To perform a t-test, clinicians will need to use a t-distribution table. A t-distribution table provides clinicians with the estimated standard deviation for a sample and is based on a specified degree of freedom (df = n-1) and a given alpha level. An abbreviated t-distribution table is shown in Table B.14.

Table B. 14

df	0.10	0.05	0.01	0.005	0.001
			p (alpha levels)		
1	3.078	6.314	31.82	63.66	318.3
2	1.886	2.920	6.965	9.925	22.33
3	1.638	2.353	4.541	5.841	10.21
4	1.533	2.132	3.747	4.604	7.173
5	1.476	2.015	3.365	4.032	5.893
6	1.440	1.943	3.143	3.707	5.208
7	1.415	1.895	2.998	3.499	4.785
8	1.397	1.860	2.896	3.355	4.501
9	1.383	1.833	2.821	3.250	4.297
10	1.372	1.812	2.764	3.169	4.144
11	1.363	1.796	2.718	3.106	4.025
12	1.356	1.782	2.681	3.055	3.930
13	1.350	1.771	2.650	3.012	3.852
14	1.345	1.761	2.624	2.977	3.787
15	1.341	1.753	2.602	2.947	3.733
16	1.337	1.746	2.583	2.921	3.686
17	1.333	1.740	2.567	2.898	3.646
18	1.330	1.734	2.552	2.878	3.611
19	1.328	1.729	2.539	2.861	3.579
20	1.325	1.725	2.528	2.845	3.552
21	1.323	1.721	2.518	2.831	3.527
22	1.321	1.717	2.508	2.819	3.505
23	1.319	1.714	2.500	2.807	3.485
24	1.318	1.711	2.492	2.797	3.467
25	1.316	1.708	2.485	2.787	3.450
26	1.315	1.706	2.479	2.779	3.435
27	1.314	1.703	2.473	2.771	3.421
28	1.313	1.701	2.467	2.763	3.408
29	1.311	1.699	2.462	2.756	3.396
30	1.310	1.697	2.457	2.750	3.385

T-distribution critical values

To compute a t-test clinicians will subtract the specified value to be tested from the sample mean and then divide the difference by the standard error of the mean. The following steps outline how to perform a single sample t-test:

Step 1. State the null and alternative hypothesis about the difference between the sample and the general population.

Step 2. Select an alpha level for the test.

Step 3. Compute the degree of freedom (n-1).

Step 4. Compute the sample mean.

Step 5. Compute the sample standard deviation.

Step 6. Subtract the hypothesized difference from the sample mean computed in step 4 ($\bar{x}$- Δ).

Step 7. Compute the square root of the sample size. ($\sqrt{n}$)

Step 8. Divide the standard deviation from step 5 by the square root of the sample size found in step 7. ($s/\sqrt{n}$)

Step 9. Divide the difference obtained in step 6 by the quotient found in step 8.

Step 10. Find the critical value where the degree of freedom intersects the selected alpha level on the t-distribution table.

Step 11. Compare the answer from step 9 with the critical value selected in step 10. If the t-test value is higher than the critical value, the null hypothesis can be rejected.

EXAMPLE: Clinicians wanted to determine with 95 percent accuracy if the average length of the stay for patients with congestive heart failure would be no more than six days. Fifteen patients were selected at random from all patients with congestive heart failure. Perform a one sample single-tailed t-test. The length of stay for the randomly selected patients were 2, 13, 3, 3, 8, 6, 6, 10, 2, 2, 11, 12, 2, 6, and 12 days.

Step 1. Hypothesis: $H_0 > 6$ day. $H_1 \leq 6$ day.

Step 2. Alpha level = 0.05

Step 3. df = 15-1 =

Step 4. 2+13+3+3+ 8+6+6+10+2+2+11+12+2+6+ 12 = /15 =

Step 5. s =

Step 6.   =

Step 7. Square root of 15 =

Step 8. / =

Step 9. / =

Step 10. critical value =

Step 11. < The null hypothesis cannot be rejected.

Correlation Coefficient

The Pearson product moment correlation coefficient is a measure of the degree to which two variables are linearly related. This correlation can be either positive or negative and ranges in value between negative one (-1) and one (1). To compute a correlation coefficient, the mean of both variable groups must be known. Clinicians should follow this procedure:

Step 1. Compute the mean for the first variable (x).

Step 2. Compute the mean for the second variable (y).

Step 3. Arrange the variables in corresponding rows in a table.

Step 4. Subtract the answer from step 1 from each of the values in the first group of variables $(x - \bar{x})$.

Step 5. Subtract the answer from step 2 from each of the values in the second group of variables $(y - \bar{y})$.

Step 6. Multiply the results of step 4 by corresponding results from step 5.

Step 7. Add together all the products from step 6.

Step 8. Square each difference computed in step 4.

Step 9. Add together each square computed in step 8.

Step 10. Square each difference computed in step 5.

Step 11. Add together each square computed in step 10.

Step 12. Compute the square root of the sum found in step 9.

Step 13. Compute the square root of the sum found in step 11.

Step 14. Multiply the square root found in step 12 by the square root found in step 13.

Step 15. Divide the result from step 7 by the product of step 14.

Step 16. Determine the correlation between variables using Colton's rule of thumb shown below.

Correlation values	Degree of relationship
0 to 0.25 or 0 to -0.25	Little or no relationship
.25 to 0.50 or -0.25 to -0.50	Fair degree of relationship
0.50 to 0.75 or -0.50 to -0.75	Moderate to good relationship
Greater than 0.75 or less than -0.75	Very good to excellent relationship

Colton (1974) rule of thumb for determining degree of correlation.

Inferential Analysis: Scattergram

Hypothesis: The timing of physical therapy impacts the length of stay.

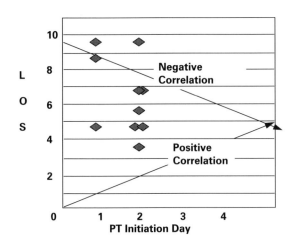

Day of P.T.	LOS (Days)
2	4
1	9
2	5
2	5
1	10
2	7
1	5
2	6
2	7
2	10

Correlation Coefficient: - 0.376
Colton Rule: Fair Degree

EXERCISE: Using the case study, determine if there is a correlation between the timing calcium channel blockers being initiated and the length of stay. (Use only the cases which are given calcium channel blockers.)

Step 1.

Step 2.

Step 3.   Arrange variables in corresponding rows in a table.

Patient	x	y	Step 4. x-$\bar{x}$	Step 5. y-$\bar{y}$	Step 6. (x-$\bar{x}$)(y-$\bar{y}$)	Step 8. (x-$\bar{x}$)^2	Step 10. (y-$\bar{y}$)^2
1							
2							
3							
4							
5							
6							
7							
8							
9							
10							
11							
12							
13							
14							
15							
16							
17							
18							
19							
20							
Sum					Step 7.	Step 9.	Step 11.

Step 12.
Step 13.
Step 14.
Step 15.
Step 16.

Summary of Inferential Tests

Statistical Test	Formula	Suggested Data Displays
Chi -Square	$x^2(df) = \sum_{\substack{all \\ cells}} \dfrac{(O - E)^2}{E}$	Table, footnote to table
Fisher Exact	$P = \dfrac{(a+b)!\,(c+d)!\,(a+c)!\,(b+d)!}{a!b!c!d!n!}$	Table, footnote to table
Single Population t-test	$t = \dfrac{\overline{x} - \Delta}{\dfrac{s}{\sqrt{n}}}$	Bell curve, footnote to table
Two Population t-test	$t = \dfrac{\overline{x_1} - \overline{x_2} - \Delta}{\sqrt{\dfrac{s_1^2}{n_1} + \dfrac{s_2^2}{n_2}}}$	Bell curves, table, line graphs, footnote to graph
Single Population z-test (mean)	$z = \dfrac{\overline{x} - \Delta}{\dfrac{\sigma}{n}}$	Bell curve, footnote to graph, line graph
Single Population z-test (proportion)	$z = \dfrac{\hat{\pi} - \pi_0}{\sqrt{\dfrac{\pi_0(1 - \pi_0)}{n}}}$	Bell curve, footnote to graph, line graph
Two Population z-test (mean)	$z = \dfrac{\overline{x_1} - \overline{x_2} - \Delta}{\sqrt{\dfrac{\sigma_1^2}{n_1} + \dfrac{\sigma_2^2}{n_2}}}$	Bell curve, table, footnote to graph, line graph
Correlation Coefficient	$r = \dfrac{\sum(X - \overline{X})(Y - \overline{Y})}{\sqrt{\sum(X - \overline{X})^2}\ \sqrt{\sum(Y - \overline{Y})^2}}$	Table, scattergraph

Inferential statistical test summary.

6

Determining Fiscal Impact of Improved Clinical Processes

Introduction

With increased awareness of health care costs and emphasis on "value added activities," quality management professionals need to be able to analyze available financial information. The reason this skill is needed is that it will help one:

- Determine the financial health of an organization
- Demonstrate the cost-benefit of quality initiatives, and
- Determine the financial impact of future clinical improvements.

Determining Financial Health

One of the skills required of all managers in health care is a basic understanding of financial reports, such as cash flow statements, balance sheets and income statements. By being able to interpret these three reports, quality management professionals can assess the health of an organization.

Financial Statements Present the Health of the Organization

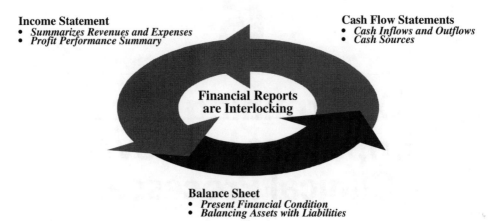

Income Statement
- *Summarizes Revenues and Expenses*
- *Profit Performance Summary*

Cash Flow Statements
- *Cash Inflows and Outflows*
- *Cash Sources*

**Financial Reports
are Interlocking**

Balance Sheet
- *Present Financial Condition*
- *Balancing Assets with Liabilities*

Cash flow statements provide information about the movement of cash, revenue sources and availability of cash. The income statement, also called a profit and loss statement, provides information about the profitability of an organization. The balance sheet presents a snapshot of the organization's financial condition at a given moment in time. The balance sheet lists all assets, including cash, accounts receivable, inventory, prepaid expenses, property, plant and equipment minus depreciation and all liabilities and equity.

Why is it important for quality professionals to know about financial statements? Simply put, quality and resources impact the bottom line of health care organizations. For example, if an organization receives most of its revenue from indemnity insurance plans, then reducing the length of stay could negatively impact the bottom line of the organization.

Hospital Anywhere: Income Statement Income Statement for One Month Ending 1/31/94		Hospital Anywhere: Income Statement Income Statement for One Month Ending 1/31/94 Adjusted for Length of Stay Reduction	
Service Revenues		**Service Revenues**	
Medicare	$1,400,000	Medicare	$1,400,000
Medicaid	$750,000	Medicaid	$750,000
Private Insurance	$2,280,000	Private Insurance	$2,052,000
HMO	$500,000	HMO	$500,000
Capitated	$750,000	Capitated	$750,000
Self	$10,000	Self	$10,000
Gross Margin	$5,690,000	**Gross Margin**	$5,461,000
Operating Expenses		**Operating Expenses**	
Wages	$2,560,500	Wages	$2,560,500
Worker's Comp & Taxes	$614,520	Worker's Comp & Taxes	$614,520
Benefits	$512,100	Benefits	$512,100
Supplies Expenses	$1,422,500	Supplies Expenses	$1,365,250
Insurance	$10,000	Insurance	$10,000
Contract Labor	$0	Contract Labor	$0
Depreciation Expenses	$112,000	Depreciation Expenses	$112,000
Mortgage	$10,000	Mortgage	$10,000
Utilities	$3,500	Utilities	$3,500
Interest Expenses	$850	Interest Expenses	$850
Total Operating Expenses	$5,245,970	**Total Operating Expenses**	$5,188,720
Net Margin Before Taxes	$444,030	Net Margin Before Taxes	$272,280
Income Taxes	$66,605	Income Taxes	$40,842
NET MARGIN	**$377,426**	**NET MARGIN**	**$231,438**

By being aware of how the income statement is computed and the organization's case mix, quality management professionals can target quality and resource activities at areas which will be mutually beneficial for patients and the organization.

Proving the Cost Benefit of Quality Initiatives

With growing emphasis on cost-containment and increasing pressure to prove "value added," many quality initiatives may be questioned in the future by administration and consumers regarding the benefits of making changes. Quality management professionals will need to answer these questions with both qualitative and quantitative data.

Some of the main reasons for analyzing the financial costs and benefits of quality initiatives include:

- Determining if a quality initiative is cost-effective
- Identifying tangible benefits
- Determining return on investment

To determine the cost benefit of a particular quality or resource initiative, the net financial benefit needs to be calculated. This calculation consists of the difference between the financial benefits and the financial costs contributed to produce the improvement result.

Financial Benefits - Costs = Cost Benefit (Net Benefit)

To start this computation process, there needs to be a review of the organizational goals for quality initiatives. The **organizational goal** is the outcome measurement for supporting the quality initiative and will answer the question "Why should I support this effort?" Organizational goals are not limited to only patient outcomes or financial contributions but will include employee and market benefits.

Organizational Goals Gives Clues for Determining Cost-Benefits

Improved patient outcomes
Improved service
Improved customer satisfaction
Improved cost effectiveness
Improved working environment
Improved competitive position

Once goals are selected for the quality initiative, the scope of costs and benefits included in the analysis should be determined. It is best to focus on short-term financial impact because these impacts are the easiest to defend and demonstrate a correlation with the quality improvement.

Exclude Long-Run Benefits in Cost Benefit Analysis: Too Many Variables

Non-financial impacts
- *Better work environment*

Financial benefits of satisfied customers
- *Don't count your chickens before they hatch*

Benefits and costs of changes made outside formal improvement initiative

Adjustments for price/cost changes, except present time
- *Can't predict the future*

Reduced staff turnover, training
- **costs, and labor grievances**
  Employee issues dependent on multiple factors

The guidelines for calculating cost benefits include:

- Select how cost and benefits will be measured. The two most common options are:

  Measuring all costs and benefits

  Using only marginal costs and benefits

- Define financial terms used in the analysis
- Specify specific inclusions and exclusions from calculations
- Determine the number of years for calculating the cost benefits
- Select a start date for calculations
- Use present value of all centralized and project costs and benefits if initiatives cover multiple years.

Terminology	Definition	Example
Financial Costs	Net marginal costs plus net revenue losses.	Reallocation of staff without experiencing an increase in payroll costs is $0.00 financial costs.
Financial Benefits	Net marginal cost savings plus net revenue increases.	If the cost of care for patients with bacterial pneumonia is decreased by $500.00 and the profit margin is increased by $200.00 then the financial benefit is $700.00 a patient.
Capital Cost Impact	Use depreciation rate as annual cost of all capital expenditures directly related to improvement.	A new computer system is purchased, depreciation is used as the capital cost impact.
Implementation Cost Impact	Length of training time X (Number of employees, physicians etc. X cost of employees time) Only additional time worked will be included.	The cost for training 200 staff nurses for 1 hour on the use of a congestive heart failure pathway resulted in 60 staff had 30 minutes of overtime. 60 X 0.5 X $37.50= $1125.00.
One-time Benefits and Costs	One time benefits and costs need to be computed for the first year benefits and costs.	A construction project is canceled because of a reduction in the emergency department waiting time makes the construction un-necessary.
Centralized Costs	Consultants, training materials, facilities and equipment, supplies, and promotion or celebration costs.	An outside consultant on how to develop critical pathways.

Terminology	Definition	Example
Centralized Benefits	Income received from speaking and consulting fees and sale of materials developed.	After developing an automated nursing documentation system for homecare, the system was marketed to other agencies.

Once the decision rules are determined, it is time to estimate the financial costs and benefits of a quality or resource initiative. An example of a cost benefit analysis is shown below.

Cost Benefit Analysis of a Pneumonia Critical Pathway

Organizational goals

- Reduce the average length of stay from six days to four days.
- Improve reimbursement
- Reduce transfers to ICU

Scope of costs and benefits (marginal)

Costs of Pathway	Benefits of Pathway
• Overtime for team meetings • Overtime for implementation training • Outside printing costs • Added staff for case management • Cost of food at meetings	• Reduction in the patient care costs • Increase in revenues • Sale of completed pathway

Pneumonia Benefit Analysis

Bacterial Pneumonia

165 Cases a year
Average cost of case: $4000.00
Average revenue per case: -$500.00
Total Loss: $82,500.00

New Pathway

165 Cases a year
Average cost per case: $3300.00
Average revenue per case: $200.00
Total profit: $33,000.00

Financial Benefits

Difference in cost of care: $700.00 per case
$700 x 165 x 2 yrs = $231,000.00

Pneumonia Cost Analysis

Marginal Cost of Developing Pathway

Overtime for Staff: $0.00
Overtime for Implementation Training: $500.00
New Equipment: $0.00
Printing Cost of Forms: $5000.00
Food Costs: $300.00

Project Costs: $5,800.00

Cost Benefit of Quality Initiative

$231,000.000 - $5,800 = $225,200

After the cost analysis is completed, a report highlighting all benefits, both tangible and intangible, needs to be written and submitted for review. The financial benefits and costs need to be reviewed by financial analysts and managers to obtain concurrence with the results.

Communicate, Communicate, Communicate

Communicate widely so costs, benefits and returns are well understood

Use multiple communication methods

7

Case Management 2000

One of the recent solutions proposed by the health care industry for managing clinical quality and resources is the concept of case management. The goal of case management is to coordinate and manage the delivery of patient care services throughout the continuum of care. Although this is a worthy goal, many of the current case management models fall short of actually achieving this objective. This chapter examines **why** these models fall short.

This chapter will focus on the requirements for developing an effective case management process and highlight strategies for changing the current case management models to meet future needs. At the conclusion of the chapter, performance improvement professionals should be able to:

- Identify current case management principles
- Describe the role case management should play in patient care, resource management and quality improvement
- Assess the benefits of a case management program in various levels of service
- Explain how case management will change during the next ten years.

Case Management Principles and Concepts

Because case management is evolutionary, there is frequent confusion about a number of issues:

- What is case management?

- How can case management be accomplished?
- What skills are required to perform effective case management?
- Where should the case management process be positioned within the health care system?

To start answering these questions and others, a generic definition for case management needs to be established. The case management definition that will be used in the following discussion is:

> Case management is a *collaborative process* that *coordinates* the delivery of essential services to customers in the health care system.

The current application of case management in health care organizations is through individuals, the case managers, who focus on managing a single case during an episode of care. There are several core principles which form the basis for case management. These principles include:

- **The principle of the empowered customer representative**. For case management to be successful, the individual assigned to this role needs to have the authority to make decisions and initiate actions on behalf of the patient.
- **The principle of collaboration**. Case management is not a person or a team but a process that facilitates collaboration and coordination among all providers of care.
- **The principle of flexibility.** Because patients require different amounts and types of services based on their clinical conditions, environment, social support and economic situation, case management needs to be flexible enough to meet these needs.
- **The principle of good care is cost effective care**. One of the basic beliefs of case management advocates is that by providing coordinated consistent care to customers quality will improve and costs will be reduced. The basis for this belief is that costs can be reduced without sacrificing quality and safety through the reduction of duplications, delays and oversights.
- **The principle of probability**. One of the basic tools of case management is the critical/clinical pathway. This tool is based on the analysis of aggregated practice and outcome data. By using a pathway, case managers are really applying a plan of care which has the greatest **probability** of meeting the average patient's needs.

Current Case Management Models

Currently, there are five principal case management models used in the health care system. The basic intent and required expertise for each model varies based on the environment in which case management functions are performed. The models are:

- Self-care model: This is a **health promotion** model which casts the customer as the case manager. This **educational** model focuses on preventing illness and promoting health. Because the **patient is responsible** for coordinating his or her own care, the health care team serves only as consultants.
- Primary care model: This model uses the primary care provider, generally a physician or nurse practitioner, as the case manager or gatekeeper. This model **encompasses many episodes of care and crosses different levels of care**. The intent of this model is to **provide consistent and coordinated care** to a single patient. The secondary intent is to **control clinical costs** by serving as a gatekeeper for referrals.
- Episodic care model: The episodic care model is currently the most frequently found case management model today. This model is generally facility or organizationally based and focuses on **providing efficient, cost effective care**. Currently, nurses are the predominant case managers for this model.
- Social service model: The social service model is probably the oldest type of case management found. This model focuses on **providing the environmental, financial and emotional support** required by a customer **to optimize independence and safety**. Generally this model appears in social service agencies and people with a background in social work serve as the case managers.
- Catastrophic care model: Usually, when a patient experiences a catastrophic illness or injury, their third-party payer assigns a case manager to coordinate and manage all patient services related to that condition. The intent of this model is to **control costs by finding the most economical means for providing care**. Case management services are provided **across the continuum of care** as they relate to the catastrophic condition. These case management services are provided by either the third party payer or brokered to an independent case management company.

Common case management characteristics can be discovered by reviewing the current models. These characteristics are present regardless of who is performing case management or where the function is located within the health care system. These common characteristics are:

1. Case management is patient focused.

2. It involves coordination of services provided to a patient.

3. It is by nature collaborative, with multiple practitioner involvement.

4. Motivation for case management is either resource or quality management.

There are several characteristics, missing in the current case management models, which need to be present to meet the changing needs of the health care system. These missing ingredients for successful case management are:

1. Holistic approach to patients' health, instead of episodic attention to illness. By converting the focus of case management from disease control to wellness promotion, longitudinal benefits can be realized.

2. A systems approach to case management which is based on aggregated clinical and financial data analysis instead of antedotal case management notes.

By combining the strengths from each of the existing case management models with the additional characteristics noted above, a new health coordination model emerges. This model focuses on providing coordinated health care services throughout a patient's life. The goal is to optimize a person's health through preventative efforts and coordinated care, thus producing long-term savings instead of short term gains.

As capitated programs expand and information management technologies develop, this model will become feasible. Also, case management programs will move from being strictly institution based to health-network based, supporting a truly coordinated health care system.

Case Management Skills

After reviewing case management principles and the available case management models it is clear that a variety of skills are required to successfully implement a case management program. These skills include:

- Clinical expertise
- Project management skills
- Communication skills
- Resource management skills
- Problem solving ability
- Data management skills
- Cost analysis ability

Because of the variety of skills required for successful case management, it is best to have a case management team rather than an individual case manager.

A possible composition of a case management team is a clinical case manager with the clinical expertise to collaborate in clinical care coordination, a resource case manager, with the expertise to manage the financial aspects of the patient and an information management specialist who can supply the cost benefit and aggregated clinical process and outcome data required for continued improvement. Each case team would support several physicians and nurse practitioners, who still retain the primary responsibility for patient care.

Future Principles of Successful Case Management

1. Future case management will be a collaborative, team oriented, patient-focused process. It will bring together teams with a multitude of disparate skills to provide seamless care episodes for patients across the entire continuum of care. The unit of case management will be the case team.

2. The degree of case management intensity will vary by case complexity. Case complexity is influenced by the type of illness or

procedure, how many points of service are involved and the intensity of services needed.

3. Case team constituency is variable and determined by the type of case being considered. The team will usually be led by a physician, although for certain types of cases, other team leaders may be more effective, such as a nurse practitioner or psychologist.

4. Case managers will act as a single point of contact or patient representative in cases of great complexity. The role would be one of coordination, patient advocacy and communication within the case management team.

Appendix A: Forms

Readiness Assessment Exercise

Directions: After reading the statement in the first column, select the level of performance which most closely matches your current knowledge, skills and abilities. Mark your answer in the appropriate box with a number one (1). After responding to all the statements in each section, add each column up and record the total on the bottom row for each column.

Clinical Study Design

Knowledge, Skills and Abilities	Proficient	Able to Perform	Need Assistance to Perform
1. Develop a clinical study			
2. State purpose of a study			
3. Formulate a hypothesis			
4. Identify data elements required to test hypothesis			
5. Select best methodology for study			
6. Determine appropriate sample size			
7. Select appropriate statistical analysis methods			
TOTAL FOR EACH COLUMN			

Data Analysis

Knowledge, Skills and Abilities	Proficient	Able to Perform	Need Assistance to Perform
1. Differentiate between geometric mean and arithmetic mean			
2. Calculate a standard deviation			
3. Create a cumulative distribution chart for a data set			
4. Calculate the chi-square for a sample population			
5. Identify the type of data required to perform a correlation coefficient test			
6. Create a control chart			
TOTAL FOR EACH COLUMN			

Financial Analysis Skills

Knowledge, Skills and Abilities	Proficient	Able to Perform	Need Assistance to Perform
1. Differentiate the purpose of a balance sheet from a profit/loss sheet			
2. Identify the factors included in a cost-benefit analysis			
3. Calculate a return on investment			
4. Recognize factors to be excluded from cost-benefit analysis			
5. Identify centralized financial costs.			
6. Define a qualitative benefit			
TOTAL FOR EACH COLUMN			

Project Management

Knowledges, Skills and Abilities	Proficient	Able to Perform	Need Assistance to Perform
1. Create a project plan			
2. Identify tasks and component parts			
3. Plan resource allocation			
4. Define critical pathway as used in a project			
5. Identify the four adjustments a project manager can make if a project is behind schedule.			
6. Describe how project milestones are spaced			
TOTAL FOR EACH COLUMN			

Data Management

Knowledge, Skills and Abilities	Proficient	Able to Perform	Need Assistance to Perform
1. Use an automated spreadsheet to calculate a standard, deviation			
2. Conduct a data base query			
3. Write specifications for information management needs			
4. Develop a presentation using at least one graphic package			
5. Produce a document which contains a table using a word-processing package			
6. Function in at least one operating environment			
TOTAL FOR EACH COLUMN			

Engineering Principles

Knowledge, Skills and Abilities	Proficient	Able to Perform	Need Assistance to Perform
1. Develop a case for action argument			
2. Create a reengineering vision			
3. Differentiate between continuous quality improvement and re-engineering			
4. Differentiate between functions and processes			
5. Identify the five key players in reengineering efforts			
6. Identify common pitfalls of reengineering			
TOTAL FOR EACH COLUMN			

Miscellaneous Skills

Knowledge, Skills and Abilities	Proficient	Able to Perform	Need Assistance to Perform
1. Facilitate a behavioral change in a clinician			
2. Convert conflict into problem-solving in a group situation			
3. Diffuse an irate customer within five minutes			
4. Teach how to perform any task to another staff member			
5. Facilitate a quality improvement team			
6. Write an action plan for correcting a JCAHO deficiency			
TOTAL FOR EACH COLUMN			

OVERALL ASSESSMENT

Directions: Copy the totals for each assessment section in the appropriate spaces listed below. Add each column and record the total in the row designated for column total. Multiply this total by the number in the multiple column and record the product in the last row. Add all point totals together and compare to key.

Skill Category	Proficient	Able to Perform	Need Assistance to Perform
Clinical Study Design			
Data Analysis			
Financial Analysis			
Project Management			
Data Management			
Reengineering Principles			
Miscellaneous			
TOTAL FOR EACH COLUMN			
MULTIPLE	X 3	X 2	X 1
TOTAL POINTS			

GRAND TOTAL: _____

Key: 119-126 = You're ready for the future
           105-118 = You have great potential
            63 -104 = With a little work you'll be there
            42 - 62 = Hard work can catch you up

Paired-Choice Matrix

Financial Analysis Forms

Diagnosis	199? Adm.	Our Avg. LOS	Target LOS	Org. Avg. Cost	Target Cost	Annual Loss

Decision Matrix Form

Potential Topics	Selection Criteria							Total	Priority Rank

Resource *Case Manager Data Sheet*

Patient Outcomes:	Demographic Information
LOS:	Admit Date: _____ D/C Date: _____
Complications: _____	Pathway: _____
Other: _____	Working Diagnosis: _____
	Procedures: _____
☐ No variance noted in the case	☐ Patient not on pathway

Addressograph Imprint

Patient Codes	System Codes	Practitioner Codes	Action Codes
P1: Patient condition	S1: Availability of test results	C1: Omit pathway intervention	A1: Request additional information
P2: Patient/Family decision	S2: Availability of space	C2: Perform additional intervention	A2: Request change in orders
P3: Patient/Family availability	S3: Availability of working equipment (Sfty)	C3: Perform pathway intervention early	A3: Provide staff education
P4: Patient/ Family actions	S4: Availability of discharge placement	C4: Delay in response time	A4: Obtain functioning equipment
P5: Patient/ Family ability to perform activity	S5: Communication breakdown	C5: Improper performance of intervention (RM)	A5: Contact another practitioner
P6: Non-compliance	S6: Availability of services	C6: Substitution of pathway intervention	A6: Reschedule intervention
P7: Change in diagnosis	S7: Availability of supplies	C7: Change in diagnosis	A7: Discontinue pathway
P8: Infectious process (IC)	S8: Availability of medications	C8: Other	A8: No action taken
P9: Other	S9: Availability of practitioner		A9: Other
	S10: Other		

Case Management Plan:

Instructions: Record the date of each variance from the pathway, the pathway element number, the variance code, corresponding actions, any additional comments and your initials in the appropriate space listed below. If no variances are noted in the case, check the box below **patient outcomes.**

Date	Function of Care	Pathway Element	Timing of Var.	Var. Code	Action Code	Comments	Reviewer's Initials

Return completed form to the Quality Management Department **within 24 hours of patient discharge.**

Pathway Data Collection Log

Pathway: _____

Date	Pt MR #	MD #	Pt Unit	Function of Care	Pathway Element	Timing Var.	Variance Code	Action Code	Comments	Patient Outcomes

Pathway Data Analysis Sheet

Pathway: _____   **Pathway Element:** _____

Date	MR#	Last Name	MD#	Chronological Segments of Care										Comments	Outcomes Measures

Critical Pathway Proposal Form

Purpose: The purpose of this form is the coordination of all pathway development and implementation activities by the Continuous Quality Improvement Steering Council.

Directions: When completed, please submit this form to the CQI Steering Council.

Initiated by: Name: _____   Extension: _____

1. Proposed Pathway Topic:

2. Describe reasons for selecting this patient population for pathway development:

3. Pathway Boundaries: (When will the pathway begin and when will the pathway end)

4. Anticipated benefits for developing and implementing this pathway:

5. Team membership:

    Leaders:

    Physician Advisor:

    Members:

6. Completion time frame: Start date (first team meeting) _____
                                         Completion date: _____

For Continuous Quality Improvement Steering Committee use
(do not write below this line)

Date received:_____

Date of team's presentation to Committee:_____
Proposal disposition:
❑ Approved as submitted   ❑ Approved as modified   ❑ Returned
for revision   ❑ Approval denied   ❑ Other
Teams reports to CQI Steering Council will be: ❑ Monthly   ❑ Quarterly

❑ Other: _____

First report scheduled for (date): _____

Critical Pathway Project Management Plan

Directions: This project management plan was developed to assist pathway teams with the development and implementation process. Complete this questionnaire and return it to the Continuous Quality Improvement Steering Council.

Step 1: Selection of Pathway Population:

A. Rationale for developing a pathway for this patient population. (Why did you select this patient population for pathway development?)

B. Results of available data review. (What data lead you to select this patient population for pathway development?)

See Initial Data Review Section

C. Patient population selected for pathway development. (Describe the patient group which is being targeted in this pathway.)

D. Pathway boundaries for selected pathway. (The points of service where the pathway begins and where the pathway ends.)

E. Pathway team members:
Leader:
Physician advisor:
Members:

Step 2: Development of Pathway

A. What are the established pathway goals: (Goals should be patient outcome focused.)

B. What external references did the team review when developing the pathway?

C. What hypotheses or assumptions did the team make about how to meet the established pathway goals. (These educated guesses should show the relationships between clinical practice and patient outcomes.)

See section labeled "Pathway Hypothesis and Analysis Plan"

D. What data was collected on current practice patterns? (Attach your baseline data collection form.)

See section labeled "Data Collection Mechanism"

E. What did analysis of data show about the relationships between clinical interventions and patient outcomes? (Attach graphs and data reports.)

See section labeled "Data Analysis"

F. What is the formulated critical pathway? (Attached a copy of the completed pathway.)

See section labeled "Clinical Pathway"

G. Who has ratified this pathway? (Groups, departments, committees, etc.)

Group Ratifying	Date of Ratification

Step 3: Implementation of Pathway

A.   What is your implementation schedule for this pathway? Complete the following table.

Implementation Activity	Responsible Party	Target Date
Pilot study of pathway 1. Provide education for staff involved in pilot study 2. Initiate pilot study of ten cases 3. Collect pilot study data 4. Analyze data 5. Revise pathway based on pilot study		
Ratification of pathway 1. 2. 4. 5. 6. 7. 8. 9. 10. 11.		

Implementation Activity	Responsible Party	Target Date
Develop a Pathway of Communication Materials 1. Create medical records forms (if appropriate) 2. Create pathway forms 3. Type pathway forms 4. Print forms		
Pre-printed physician orders 1. Write orders 2. Type orders 3. Obtain signatures for file		
Development of pathway instructions and key term definitions 1. Review current pathway policy and procedures 2. Create specific instructions 3. Define key terms which are unique to this pathway 4. Type specific instructions 5. Print specific instructions		
Development of Patient Education Materials 1. Identify pathway elements for patient pathway 2. Create patient educational material 3. Type final patient education materials 4. Print patient education materials		
Staff education about pathway 1. Design staff education program 2. Prepare educational materials 3. Schedule inservices 4. 5. 6. 7. 8. 9. 10. 11. 12. 13. 14.		

Implementation Activity	Responsible Party	Target Date
Report Results of Pathway 1. Involved departments 2. Continuous Quality Improvement Council 3. Medical executive committee 4. Establish frequency of reporting		
Identify Triggers for Pathway Revision 1. Practioner 2. Institutional 3. Community		

Step 4: Measurements of Pathway Results
A. What data is to be collected?

B. Who will collect data?

C. When will data be collected?

D. Who will analyze the collected data?

E. Where should the collected data be reported?

F. What is the frequency for reporting the collected data?

Step 5: Utilization of Pathway Results
A. How will compliance with the pathway be reinforced?

B. What information will trigger pathway revisions?

Determining Pathway Readiness

Step 1. Using the category stated in the first column, list your organization's possible issues which will prohibit or limit pathway success. Record these issues in the second column.

Step 2. As a group share these issues and develop a plan for addressing these identified issues and record these in the third column.

Pathway Requirement	Identified Issues Which Will Impede Pathway Process	Proposed Plan for Addressing Issues
Upper Management Support		
Medical Staff Involvement		
Clinician Support		

Pathway Requirement	Identified Issues Which Will Impede Pathway Process	Proposed Plan for Addressing Issues
Organizational Performance Improvement Foundation		
Communication System		
Information Management Systems		
Time		

Glossary of Terms

AHCPR: Agency for Health Care Policy and Research.

Case Management Plan: A tentative course of action used to measure and manage patient care activities.

Care Manager: The individual assigned to measure and manage a specific patient's critical pathway activities. This term is synonymous with clinical case manager.

Case Manager: The individual assigned to measure and manage a specific patient's critical pathway activities, perform utilization review and coordinate discharge planning.

Clinical Pathway: Every element of care required on a daily basis throughout an episode of treatment, regardless of the impact on patient outcomes.

Critical Pathway Guide: A written copy of a critical pathway used to provide direction for clinical interventions and documentation of care. This guide can be a temporary or permanent part of the medical record.

Clinical Practice Guidelines: Statements which describe appropriate health care decisions and activities for a specific clinical condition. These statements can be developed by professional, regulatory, commercial or educational groups.

Clinician: Any individual who provides clinical care to patients. This term is used synonymously with caregiver and practitioner. For example, physicians, nurses and social workers are all practitioners.

Cluster Random Sample: A two stage sampling process which first sub-divides the population into groups or clusters according to a specific characteristic, then a random sample of clusters is chosen. A portion of subjects within each cluster are selected. This sampling method is most often used in epidemiological research and commonly based on geographic areas or districts.

Concurrent Review: The process on monitoring the care provided to patients during an episode of care. This term is synonymous with prospective review.

Consensus: A group decision that all members of the group accept and support.

CQI: Continuous Quality Improvement.

Criteria: Standards or rules on which a judgment or decision can be based.

Critical Pathway: The few vital clinical activities in a treatment regimen proven to have an impact on the clinical or financial outcomes of care.

Decision Matrix: A decision support tool used to rank several options relative to a set of criteria.

Dependent Variable: An element in a study the value of which is changed by the presence or absence of one or more other variables.

External Data Source: The point outside an organization where information originates.

External Triggers: Conditions or events outside the organization that precipitate an evaluation and/or revision of the current critical pathway.

Independent Variable: A factor in a study that is unchanged by the presence or absence of other variables.

Internal Data Source: The point within an organization where information is created.

Internal Triggers: Conditions or events within the organization that precipitate an evaluation and/or revision of the current critical pathway.

Matrix: An array of data shown in columns and rows.

Opportunity Statement: A concise statement to describe a process in need of improving, its boundaries, the reasons for concern and the expected benefits of improving the process.

Pathway Boundaries: The points of service where a pathway starts and where it ends.

Pathway Hypothesis: A statement describing a clinician's beliefs or educated guesses about the relationship between specific clinical elements and outcomes.

Patient Care Review Activities: The traditional clinical monitoring functions found in a health care organization. These functions include quality assurance and control, utilization review, risk management and infection control.

Patient Variance: A deviation from the critical pathway caused by a change in the patient's condition, or due to the availability, decisions or actions of the patient or his or her significant other.

Point of Service: A specific moment of time when a particular department or branch of a health care organization's staff provides specified patient care.

Practice Parameters: Elements of care promulgated by professional societies, regulatory agencies or published in literature which define the boundaries of safe clinical practice.

Practitioner: Any individual who provides clinical care to patients. This term is used synonymously with caregiver and clinician. Physicians, nurses and social workers (among others) are all practitioners.

Practitioner Variance: A deviation from the critical pathway caused by an omission or commission by a caregiver without evidence of a system or patient variance.

Pre-printed Physician Orders: Physician orders which are pre-printed but must be activated by a physician order.

QTA: Quality Team Associates.

Retrospective Review: The process of monitoring the care provided to patients after an episode of care is complete.

Scope of Pathway: The range of patient care services provided within the boundaries of a pathway.

Standards of Care: The level of assistance or treatment provided to those in need.

Standards of Practice: The level of performance demonstrated during the assistance or treatment of those in need.

Standing Orders: Diagnostic and treatment protocols which are activated without a physician's order.

Simple Random Sample: A portion of items (cases) selected from a population in a manner which ensures all items have an equal chance or probability of being chosen.

Skill Assessment: An evaluation of the knowledge, skills and abilities required to perform a task.

Stratified Random Sample: Selecting a portion of a population by sub-dividing it according to specified characteristics, then randomly choosing cases from each sub-group.

Systematic Random Sample: A sampling method where every nth number of items is selected for the sample. "N" is a predetermined constant number of cases. For example, every seventh case will be included in the sample.

System Variance: A deviation from the critical pathway caused by breakdown or unavailability of services, information, supplies, medications or equipment.

Variance: Any deviation from the critical pathway schedule of clinical assessments and interventions regardless of its impact on patient outcomes.

Bibliography and References

Agency of Health Care Policy and Research. *Clinical Practice Guidelines,* U.S. Department of Health and Human Services, 1993.

American Heritage Dictionary. 3d ed. (1992).

Association for Practitioners in Infection Control. *The APIC Curriculum for Infection Control Practice*, 3 Vols. Dubuque: Kendall/Hunt, 1983. Vol. I.

Batalden, Paul and Buchanan, David. "Hospital Quality: Patient, Physician and Employee Judgments." *International Journal of Health Care Quality Assurance.* (Nov. 1990): 7-17.

Berwick, Donald M. "Sounding Board: Continuous Improvement as an Ideal in Health Care." *New England Journal of Medicine.* 320:1. (Jan. 1989): 53-56.

Chang, Richard Y., and Kelly, P. Keith, *Step-By-Step Problem Solving*, Richard Chang Associates, Inc., Irvine, 1993.

Coile, Russel C. Jr. "Future Trends, Health Care Reform and the Outlook for Long-Term Care," *Journal of Long-Term Care Administration* (Fall 1993): 6-10.

Cook, Thomas D. and Campbell, Donald T., *Quasi-Experimentation: Design & Analysis Issues for Field Settings,* Boston, 1979.

Cribbing, James J. *Leader Skills for Executives.* Boston: Education for Management, Inc., 1977.

Dawson-Saunders, Beth, and Trapp, Robert G. *Basic & Clinical Biostatistics,* Norwalk: Appleton & Lange, 1994.

Donabedian, A. *Exploration in Quality Assessment and Monitoring.* Vol. 1, *The Definition of Quality and Approaches to Its Assessment.* Ann Arbor: Health Administration Press, 1980.

Donabedian, A. *Exploration in Quality Assessment and Monitoring.* Vol.2, *The Criteria and Standards of Quality.* Ann Arbor: Health Administration Press, 1982.

Donabedian, A. *Exploration in Quality Assessment and Monitoring*. Vol. 3, *The Methods and Findings of Quality Assessment Monitoring: An Illustrated Analysis*. Ann Arbor: Health Administration Press, 1985.

Doyle, Richard L., *Healthcare Management Guidelines*, 5 Vols. San Francisco, CA: Milliman & Robertson, 1992. Vol. 2: *Return-to-Work Planning*.

Fanale, James E.; Keenan, Joseph M.; Hepburn, Kenneth W.; and Von Sternberg, Thomas. "Care Management," *Journal of American Geriatrics Society* 39:4, (April 1991): 431-437.

Gitlow, Howard S. And Shelly J. *The Deming Guide to Quality and Competitive Position*. Englewood Cliffs: Prentice-Hall, 1987.

Gronlund, Norman E. *Stating Objectives for Classroom Instruction,* 2d ed. New York: Macmillan, 1978.

Howe, Rufus S. *Case Management for Healthcare Professionals*, Chicago: Precept Press, 1994.

Jader, Gary. "Ten Steps to Effective Persuasive Speaking," *Nursing Management* (March 1993): 46-48.

Joint Commission on Accreditation of Healthcare Organizations. *1994 Accreditation Manual for Hospitals Volume I*. Chicago: Joint Commission on Accreditation of Healthcare Organizations, 1993.

Juran, Joseph M. *Juran on Planning for Quality*. New York: The Free Press, 1988.

Juran, Joseph M. *Juran on Quality by Design: The New Steps for Planning Quality into Goods and Services*. New York: The Free Press, 1992.

Hammer, Michael and Champy, James. *Reengineering the Corporation: A Manifesto for Business Revolution*. New York, Harper Business. 1993.

Kongstvedt, Peter R., *The Managed Health Care Handbook*. 2d ed. Gaithersburg, MD: Aspen Publications, 1993.

Leedy, Paul D., *Practical Research Planning and Design,* New York: Macmillan, 1980.

Lewis-Ford, Brenda Kay, "Management Techniques: Coping with Difficult People," *Nursing Management,* Vol. 24 (March 1993): 36-38.

McClelland, Eleanor; Kelly, Kathleen; and Kathleen C. Buckwalter, *Continuity of Care: Advancing the Concept of Discharge Planning,* Orlando: Grune & Stratton, 1985.

Shortell, Stephen M.; Morrison, Ellen M.; and Friedman, Bernard. *Strategic Choices for America's Hospitals*, San Francisco: Jossey-Bass, 1992.

Sloan, John P. *Protocols in Primary Care Geriatrics*. New York: Springer-Verlag, 1991.

Townsend, Patrick L. And Gebhardt, J.E. *Commit to Quality.* New York: Wiley, 1986.

VHA Tri-State Inc., *Continuous Quality Improvement: Strategies & Methods*. Nashville: Hospital Corporation of America, 1991.

Wall, Deborah K., and Joseph, Eric D. *Critical Pathways: Development and Implementation A Discussion Guide* Chicago: Care Communications, 1992.

Wall, Deborah K., and Joseph, Eric D. "Guidelines for Developing Critical Pathways" *Quality Management Update* 3:5 (May 1993): 6-8.

Wall, Deborah K., and Proyect, Mitchell M. *Moving from Parameters to Pathways: A Guide for Developing and Implementing Critical Pathways* Santa Cruz: Quality Team Associates, 1994.

Wall, Deborah K., and Proyect, Mitchell M. *Issues Which Impact Critical Pathway Success* Santa Cruz: Quality Team Associates, 1994.

White House Domestic Policy Council, *The President's Health Security Plan*, New York: Times Books, 1993.

Woolf, Steven H. "Practice Guidelines: A New Reality in Medicine III. Impact on Patient Care," *Archives of Internal Medicine*. 153 (Dec. 1993): 2646-2655.

Index